PORTFOLIO / PENGUIN

INSANELY SIMPLE

Ken Segall worked closely with Steve Jobs as ad agency creative director for NeXT and Apple. He was a member of the team that created Apple's legendary *Think different* campaign, and he's responsible for that little "i" that's a part of Apple's most popular products. Segall has also served as creative director for IBM, Intel, Dell, and BMW. He blogs about technology and marketing at kensegall.com/blog, and has fun with it all at scoopertino.com. Follow Segall on Twitter: @ksegall.

Insanely Simple

The Obsession That Drives Apple's Success

Ken Segall

Portfolio/Penguin

PORTFOLIO/PENGUIN
Published by the Penguin Group
Penguin Group (USA) Inc., 375 Hudson Street,
New York, New York 10014, USA

USA | Canada | UK | Ireland | Australia | New Zealand | India | South Africa | China
Penguin Books Ltd, Registered Offices: 80 Strand, London WC2R oRL, England
For more information about the Penguin Group visit penguin.com

First published in the United States of America by Portfolio/Penguin, a member of Penguin Group
(USA) Inc. 2012
This paperback edition with a new chapter published 2013

THE LIBRARY OF CONGRESS HAS CATALOGED THE HARDCOVER EDITION AS FOLLOWS:
Segall, Ken.
Insanely simple : the obsession that drives Apple's success / Ken Segall.
p.   cm.
Includes index.
ISBN 978-1-59184-483-9 (hc.)
ISBN 978-1-59184-621-5 (pbk.)
1. Creative ability in business.   2. Marketing.   3. Apple Computer, Inc.   4. Jobs, Steve, 1955–
2011.   I. Title.
HD53.S44 2012
658.4'094—dc23
2011049212

Printed in the United States of America
ScoutAutomatedPrintCode

Set in Adobe Garamond Pro with Myriad Pro
Designed by Daniel Lagin

For Jeremy,
Simply the best kid a dad could have

Contents

"Simplify, simplify."
—Henry David Thoreau

"Simplify."
—Apple

Preface

Life is a combination of skill and luck. I won't claim to be the most skilled person in my profession, but I'm definitely one of the luckiest. Between NeXT and Apple, I got to work with Steve Jobs for over a decade.

It wasn't always easy. It might not even have been healthy. But it was always exciting, and I'll forever be in Steve's debt for the lessons I learned.

Steve passed away before I finished this book. Though his death was expected, part of me refused to expect it. I secretly clung to the hope that maybe, possibly, his health was better than it appeared. I didn't want to think of the world without him.

So in addition to its original business purpose, this book has taken on a personal meaning. I wish to pay tribute to Steve—for all he's contributed to the world and for the opportunities he gave me personally.

I didn't invent the concepts in this book. I merely observed them. Thank you, Steve, for making things so simple.

Insanely Simple

Introduction
The Simple Stick

Apple's package-design team had just returned from their presentation to Steve Jobs, and their faces told the story. There were no visible signs of carnage. They just had that "things didn't go exactly as we planned" look.

I felt bad for them, because I knew they'd been pouring their hearts into a project for several weeks, trying to solve a thorny packaging issue. I was working on an unrelated project in the building and had been invited into their high-security, hermetically sealed chamber at several points to join the brainstorming.

While the team was decompressing after their Steve meeting, I crossed paths with the project leader in the creative group's kitchen.

"The suspense is killing me," I said. "How'd it go this morning?"

"Well," he said, "Steve hit us with the Simple Stick."

Translation: Steve had rejected their work—not because it was bad but because in some way it failed to distill the idea to its essence. It took a turn when it should have traveled a straight line.

In this case it hadn't even been the creative effort that bothered Steve—it was the project itself. The person leading the project had directed the team to create packaging for two versions of the same product. Steve had decided this was brain-dead. "Just combine them," he said. "One product, one box." There was no need to explore the idea of a second package.

He was right. It was simpler, quicker, better. The conversation was over in minutes, and it left one very smart and talented group of people wondering why they hadn't thought of that before.

The Simple Stick symbolizes a core value within Apple. Sometimes it's held up as inspiration; other times it's wielded like a caveman's club. In all cases, it's a reminder of what sets Apple apart from other technology companies and what makes Apple stand out in a complicated world: a deep, almost religious belief in the power of Simplicity.

As those who have worked with Apple will attest, the simpler way isn't always the easiest. Often it requires more time, more money, and more energy. It might require you to step on a few toes. But more times than not, it will lead to measurably better results.

Simplicity has been a driving force at Apple since the earliest days of the two Steves, Jobs and Wozniak. It inspired them to create a computer that could actually help a human being accomplish something wonderful—as opposed to just processing data in the dark basement of some faceless corporation.

And of course Simplicity was the guiding light for Macintosh, which introduced the biggest leap in the history of computers: a graphical interface controlled by a mouse. (Now, don't get all technical with me about who *really* invented this. Macintosh was the first computer to popularize it.)

When Steve Jobs took the stage to announce Macintosh in 1984, he used words that would resonate for decades to come. He called it "insanely great."

It was the kind of insanity that caused people to line up around the block to get a closer look at this technology milestone. When Steve returned to Apple after eleven years in exile, so did the insanity—and the lines started forming once again. First he reignited computers (iMac), then he revolutionized music (iPod and iTunes), then smartphones (iPhone), and most recently computers all over again (iPad).

Every one of Apple's revolutions was born of the company's devotion to Simplicity. Each new device either created a new category or turned an existing category on its head—all because, as an old iMac ad put it, the technology was "simply amazing, and amazingly simple."

Having played a lead role in the marketing of Intel, Dell, and IBM, as well as Apple, I can assure you that Apple's focus on Simplicity is unique. It goes beyond enthusiasm, beyond passion, all the way to obsession.

While Apple's love of Simplicity started in the mind of Steve Jobs, it's now burned deep into the company's DNA, serving as a guide for legions of employees around the world. It pays off in the satisfaction that comes with sparking revolution after revolution. It also pays off in a more traditional way—with massive piles of cash.

To appreciate that, you need only look at the size of Apple's profits versus those of any one competitor. Better yet, look at the size of Apple's profits versus those of all of its competitors combined. In the second quarter of 2012, Apple's 6.5 percent of the global handset market accounted for about 75 percent of the industry's total operating profit. In PCs, Apple's small market share (about 5 percent worldwide) also rakes in a greatly disproportionate percentage of the total industry's profits.

By no means am I saying that Simplicity is the sole factor behind Apple's success. Leadership, vision, talent, imagination, and incredibly hard work may have just a bit to do with it. But there's one common thread that runs through it all. That's Simplicity. It's what drives Apple to create what it creates and behave as it behaves. It's Apple's devotion to Simplicity that forms an unbreakable connection with its customers and inspires customers to evangelize to colleagues, friends, and family.

Simplicity not only enables Apple to revolutionize—it enables Apple to revolutionize *repeatedly*. As the world changes, as technology changes, as the company itself adapts to change, the religion of Simplicity is the one constant. It's the set of values that allows Apple to turn technology into devices that are just too hard to resist.

There's nothing subtle about Apple's love affair with Simplicity. It's everywhere you look. It's in the company's products, its ads, its internal organization, its stores, and its customer relationships. Inside Apple, Simplicity is a goal, a work style, and a measuring stick.

But all of this leads to a very good question: If Apple's obsession with Simplicity is so obvious, and the financial results are equally obvious, why on earth aren't other technology companies simply copying Apple's methods to achieve the same level of success?

The quick answer: It ain't easy.

Simplicity is not merely a layer that can be grafted onto a business. It isn't available in a prepackaged version. It doesn't work with an on/off switch. Yet it's there for absolutely anyone to take advantage of, if only they have the determination and knowledge.

Simplicity doesn't spontaneously spring to life with the right combination of molecules, water, and sunlight. It needs a champion—someone who's willing to stand up for its principles and strong enough to resist the overtures of Simplicity's evil twin, Complexity. It needs someone who's willing to guide a process with both head and heart.

As you can imagine, it's a lot more fun to wield the Simple Stick than it is to get whacked by it. By embracing the values of Simplicity, you will be the one who promotes change, keeps colleagues on course, and proves your value to the company day by day.

The Undeniable Truth

Since this book is about Simplicity, it's important to point out that virtually everything you read here is born of one simple fact: People prefer Simplicity.

Maybe it's a little early in the book to be quite so simple. So here's a slightly wordier version: Given the option, any sane person will choose the simple path over one that's more complicated.

If that still seems too obvious, then you're well on your way to appreciating one of Simplicity's most outstanding attributes. It looks, acts, and sounds perfectly natural. Your head involuntarily nods in agreement.

But never underestimate the degree to which people crave this kind of clarity and respond positively to it. Most of us live in a world that's become increasingly complicated, where Simplicity isn't all that easy to find. It boils down to basic supply and demand: As Simplicity becomes more rare, it also becomes more valuable. So your ability to keep things simple, and protect things from becoming more complicated, becomes more valuable as well.

People of all ages, religions, cultures, and political beliefs prefer Simplicity. In fact, it's not just human beings who prefer it. This preference is burned into the basic wiring of all living cells. When it comes to ordinary, everyday decisions, most life-forms agree: The simpler path is the far more attractive one.

Whether you're a person, dog, fish, or amoeba, you will respond more positively to the simpler solution—even if it isn't a conscious response. Businesspeople who understand, embrace, and leverage this fact are destined to achieve greater success than those who do not.

Now if everyone and everything has a built-in preference for Simplicity, why does business—and life—remain so complicated? Well, nature has this thing about "balance." While there exists this wonderful idea called Simplicity, there also exists that dark cloud called Complexity. Complexity can be powerful and seductive, so it should never be underestimated.

Its recruits often look and act just like the rest of us. You meet them just about every day in the course of your business. These people either believe or have been led to believe that their complex ways are somehow more ingenious. Sometimes it's possible to show them the light. Other times all we can do is try to defang them. In an odd way, we should be thankful that these agents of Complexity exist, for their presence makes Simplicity stand out that much more.

Simplicity is power, whether it's used by individuals or organizations. The question is, do you have the insight and skills to turn this power into your own business advantage?

You will soon.

Is This a Marketing Book or What?

This is a book about the obsession that drives Apple's success: Simplicity.

But to truly understand Simplicity—to appreciate how it's implemented, maintained, and enforced at Apple, to learn how you can use its power to achieve your company's goals—you need to see it in context. And in the organization that Steve Jobs built, marketing is the context for just about everything. It's not an exaggeration to say that marketing is as critical to Apple's success as the devices the company makes.

So will many of the stories I share in this book revolve around marketing? Absolutely. Will this book be helpful to you if you're in the marketing business? I'd feel wounded if it wasn't. Do you have to be in marketing to gain important business insights from this book? Not at all.

This book is about ideas and processes. It's about creating the best work and giving it the best chance of survival. It's about getting from point A to point B more efficiently and with far happier results. These principles apply to a range of businesses—certainly not just marketing.

If you engage with clients, manage a team, work against deadlines, or coordinate groups to solve thorny problems, this book will spark ideas and insights to make your business more successful, whatever your business might be.

If you're not familiar with marketing, trust me, you will hardly be intimidated by the situations described here. As you've seen in *Mad Men* and a hundred other TV shows and movies about this business, it's easy to understand. And in Apple's world, the real-life stories are at least as entertaining as the Hollywood versions.

In this book, you'll be a fly on the wall inside a conference room with Steve Jobs. You'll be on the receiving end of his midnight phone call. While many of the conversations I describe are about various facets of marketing, they'll illuminate the love of Simplicity that makes Apple Apple—and can help your business win, Apple style.

Your humble guide for this journey is an advertising creative director who spent seventeen years working in the worlds of Apple and NeXT, conspiring with others of my ilk to create the marketing campaigns that helped define these companies. It was my job to turn complicated ideas into interesting and compelling stories—a feat I will attempt to replicate in this book.

Insanely Simple's Raison d'Être

As the legend of Apple has grown, so has the stack of books written about it. Many are authored by journalists or other outsiders who've done their homework and pulled together disparate stories from the inside.

This isn't that kind of book.

The operative theory here is that, while Apple does many things well—hardware, software, manufacturing, strategy, product launches, PR, marketing, retail, and much more—Simplicity is the common thread that ties them all together.

If you understand how Simplicity has helped make Apple the most valuable company on earth, you can apply it to your own business in a hundred different ways. You can use Simplicity to separate your business from the pack in much the same way that Apple has used it to eclipse its competitors.

To be honest, Apple was not the only inspiration for this book. As a writer who caught technology fever long ago, I toiled for many years creating campaigns for other iconic companies, including IBM, Intel, and Dell. It was the stark contrast between Apple's culture and the cultures of the others that made me appreciate the power of Simplicity. On one side I saw a company rising on the wings of Simplicity; on the other I could see companies losing everyday struggles against Complexity. Across the board I saw companies that showed an interest in Simplicity—but only one made it an obsession. And only one rose to such astronomical heights.

I not only had the opportunity to compare Apple to other companies but was able to compare Apple to its former self. That's because in addition to serving the Steve Jobs administration, I was a creative director at Apple's agency during the dark days when John Sculley reigned as CEO. I also had the opportunity to work with two different versions of Steve Jobs: one at NeXT, the other at Apple.

Selected experiences from all of these times are distilled into this book. My goal is to present a diverse selection of stories that together define the obsession that drives Apple's success. I do this in the hope that it can also drive your company's success.

What Makes Simplicity Tick

For a concept that's supposed to be obvious, Simplicity can be difficult to describe. It can be a choice, a feeling, or a guiding light. You might even think of it as a spirit, for you can tell pretty quickly when you're in a place that believes in it and when you're in a place that doesn't.

Simplicity is the love child of two of the most powerful forces in business: Brains and Common Sense.

Since most people are endowed with both, you'd think that Simplicity would rule the world. Unfortunately, that's not the case. For example, Common Sense would suggest that when Microsoft created the Zune Store to compete with the iTunes Store, it would have charged a fixed price per song, much as Apple did. Instead, it offered "Microsoft Points," which required customers to purchase points by the hundred, then use a conversion rate of eighty points to the dollar to buy a ninety-nine-cent song. The architect of that scheme seems to be missing the Common Sense gene—and those who approved it were a bit light in the Brains department.

No, the fact is that Brains and Common Sense often go AWOL in this world, even inside companies that were founded on sheer smarts, like Microsoft. Once again, that's because Simplicity has its own kryptonite in the equal and opposite force of Complexity. If one were to judge by the balance we currently see in this world, a strong argument could be made that Complexity may even be the stronger of the two.

It is because of the existence of Complexity, and the safe haven it finds all around us, that even those with the best of intentions—well stocked with Brains and Common Sense—sometimes fail in their quest for Simplicity.

Simplicity and Complexity have been locked in mortal combat since the dawn of civilization. And Complexity, unfortunately, is part of the human condition. It lives inside all of us—yes, including people like Steve Jobs. By the end of this book, you'll see that even Steve, champion of Simplicity, was perfectly capable of lapsing and falling victim, if only momentarily, to the Complexity within.

Unlike Simplicity, which normally presents itself with a certain elegance, Complexity can get ugly. Even worse, it can never die. But the good news is, neither can Simplicity. It's capable of defeating any challenge from the dark side—it just needs someone to fight on its behalf.

Happily, you don't have to start from scratch. You can take some lessons from the company that wrote the book on Simplicity. Like Apple, you can use the power of Simplicity to get noticed in a complicated world.

Your competitors may be bigger or better funded—but you'll have the Simple Stick.

Prepare for Battle

Over years of meetings with Steve Jobs and his Apple marketing team, it was obvious that I was working in a special place. So I made it a habit to put an asterisk in my notes when something memorable happened or a key decision was made. I wanted to bookmark the things that made Apple different from other companies I'd worked with.

When I looked back at my notes, I thought there were way too many asterisks to make any sense of them. However, when my harvest was complete, I realized that just about every one of these moments in some way reflected Apple's obsession with Simplicity. Though Apple applies its obsession in many different ways, the moments I recorded formed a pattern. Ten core elements of Simplicity seemed to emerge.

These elements aren't trademarked by Apple or anyone else. They belong to all of us. Apple may be the world's greatest practitioner of Simplicity, but there's room for everyone to play.

If you're prepared to do battle with Complexity, you'll have no trouble finding a fight. Chances are, you're surrounded by it. Unless you work in the rarest of environments, Complexity lives inside your organization's hierarchy, its goals, and probably most of your colleagues as well. If your company is ever to fail, you can be sure it won't be the fault of Simplicity—it will be the result of its absence.

In each chapter of this book, I will focus on one core element of Simplicity and show you how Steve Jobs's and Apple's deep devotion to it led them to act as they did. By book's end, you'll understand how all these elements fit together, and you'll be armed with a powerful weapon to move your business forward.

Just understand that Simplicity is more than a goal—it's a skill. To successfully leverage its power, you need to get good at it. That takes practice. And this is where things get a little tricky. Because the irony is, becoming skilled in Simplicity isn't that simple. You can't just learn it; you need to make it second nature.

As important, you must understand that Simplicity is not a smorgasbord from which you can pick and choose at whim. You buy the whole thing or you buy none of it. Because if your understanding or skills are incomplete, you'll be no match for Complexity, which knows every trick in the book.

Chapter 1
Think Brutal

Steve Jobs was waiting in the conference room on the other side of the building, and I imagined he wanted to kill me.

It wasn't my fault. I hadn't done anything. I'd simply resigned from one of the most coveted jobs in advertising—creative director at Apple's ad agency in Los Angeles—to take the job in New York as the agency creative director for Steve's new computer company, NeXT.

Only problem was, nobody thought to have Steve interview me before I was hired, and apparently he wasn't too pleased about that.

So my head was filled with nervous thoughts as I made the trek across the building to my first agency meeting with Steve. I wasn't scared enough that my life flashed before me. However, I was scared enough that I was busy thinking of a contingency plan in case this meeting fulfilled its potential for disaster.

My new agency was the creatively acclaimed Ammirati & Puris, which was well known and admired for its work on BMW. It was Ralph Ammirati himself who welcomed me on the scene and gave me the heads-up about his little faux pas with Steve. He was sure we would get past this glitch, but his confidence only made me figure he had a good replacement creative director in mind. Certainly many would have jumped at the opportunity. Steve Jobs was no longer at Apple, but his fame and charisma were perfectly intact.

I hadn't worked with Steve before, but I did feel a connection. My mentor and boss on Apple back in Los Angeles was Steve Hayden, the man responsible for introducing the Macintosh computer when he worked at the ad agency Chiat/Day. He was the author of Apple's *1984* commercial, the spot that turned the Super Bowl into a grand advertising event and is thought by many to be the greatest commercial ever made. I'd heard many stories from Hayden about working with Steve Jobs, and now I would be having those adventures firsthand. Assuming I survived the next hour.

Oddly, I had to move from Los Angeles to New York for this opportunity, even though NeXT was based just south of San Francisco. Steve had chosen Ammirati & Puris simply because he demanded the best. He had become enamored of the advertising for both BMW ("The ultimate driving machine") and UPS ("We run the tightest ship in the shipping business") and instructed his marketing people to find the agencies that did these things. Once he learned that a single agency had created both, Ammirati quickly became his agency of record.

So with an ever-quickening heartbeat, I walked that long hallway to the conference room, where I took a deep breath and opened the door. There stood Steve, chatting it up with Ralph, who waved me over for the official introduction. Steve gave me a welcoming smile. Our conversation started while we were still shaking hands.

"So, I hear you've been doing the ads for Apple," he said.

I took that as a hopeful sign. Maybe he thought of me as a kindred spirit.

"Yep," I said proudly. After all, we'd won a ton of awards.

"I really like the TV you've been doing," Steve said, giving my confidence another boost. Then, still looking me right in the eye and engaging me with his warmest smile, he added, "The print is really shit."

It was one of those moments when you can't quite figure out what you're supposed to do, and you have but a second to figure it out. For reasons unknown, I strained mightily to keep my happy smile going.

"Thanks," was all I could muster, realizing I had just thanked the man for telling me that my work sucked. But somehow it was okay. There wasn't any malice in Steve's words; he was just being himself, and I was happy that at least the ice was broken, even though part of my ego was broken as well. I suddenly felt like I was going to get my opportunity to succeed or fail on my own merit.

To be honest, it wasn't until years later that I thought back on this first encounter and realized how beautifully it foretold so many future meetings. I didn't think of Steve in terms of being nice or mean, approving or disapproving. He was simply being straight with me. The relationship we would have over the years ahead would always remain that simple. Steve didn't like Complexity in his working relationships any more than he liked extra buttons on his iPod.

Blunt is Simplicity. Meandering is Complexity.

In the coming months, I learned that what I had experienced was just the way it was with Steve. He was going to tell you what was on his mind, and he couldn't care less how you might feel about it.

Few of us have the willingness or capacity to be this honest 100 percent of the time. It's not that we're devious. It's just that in certain circumstances, we become discomfort averse. We might want to spare someone's feelings or avoid being the one to wreck the positive vibes in the room. These things were nonissues for Steve. Whether you were friend or foe, the truth was the truth and his opinion was his opinion. It had nothing to do with whether or not he liked you or valued your contribution, and it certainly had nothing to do with the mood in the room.

Having done my time with the marketing teams at Intel and Dell, I can only tell you that being on the receiving end of brutally frank talk isn't as common as you might think. Far more prevalent in the corporate world is the varnished truth, followed closely by the sporadic truth.

For example, you may hear that the CEO thought your work had fatal flaws—when in fact he had comments that could be easily addressed. What you're hearing might be more the messenger's interpretation than honest feedback. The middleman—in this case, your client—might be seeing things through the prism of his or her own agenda. So you don't get the whole truth, your team goes off to rethink the project, and as quickly as that, Complexity has burrowed into your business relationship and started to do its damage.

When you work with Apple, you know exactly where you stand, what the goals are, and how quickly you need to perform. You're also aware of the consequences should you screw up.

Clarity propels an organization. Not occasional clarity but pervasive, twenty-four-hour, in-your-face, take-no-prisoners clarity. Most people never perceive that this is lacking in their organization, but 90 percent of the time it is. Just open a few random emails on your company account, activate your brutal-vision, and read. The muddying messages are rampant. If people were brutally honest in their emails, the time we spend sorting through our in-boxes would surely decrease by half.

Steve Jobs demanded straightforward communication from others as much as he dished it out himself. He had no patience for those who beat around the bush. He'd cut you off if you rambled. He ran his business as if there were precious little time to waste, which well reflected the reality for Apple—as surely it does for any company serious about competing.

This is probably the one element of Simplicity that's easiest to institute. Just be honest and never hold back. Demand the same from those you work with. You'll make some people squirm, but everyone will know where they stand. One hundred percent of your group's time will be focused on forward progress—no need to decode what people are really saying.

There is a general perception that Steve Jobs was the nasty tyrant who demanded allegiance, barked commands, and instilled the fear of God in those around him. While Steve certainly did exhibit these behaviors, this portrait is incomplete. The man could also be funny, warm, and even charming. There is a huge difference between being brutally honest and simply being brutal.

Being straight with people does not alone make you a heartless bastard.

It does not mandate that you become manipulative or mean. It's simply a matter of saying what needs to be said to push your team to deliver the best possible results.

Standards Aren't for Bending

As human beings, few of us are immune to the emotional needs of those around us. Even if we don't say it out loud, we care. At least a little. So when we see colleagues working hard and sacrificing their personal lives for the good of the company, of course we root for them to succeed. But Simplicity has a merciless side. That is, there's no "almost" when it comes to making things simpler.

Apple's longtime agency Chiat/Day is so well known for its clever T-shirts that it once published a "best of" book. One of its more famous T-shirts attempted to fight off the human instinct to settle for near perfection. It read, "Good enough is not enough."

For Steve Jobs, that T-shirt wasn't nearly tough enough. His standards simply weren't negotiable. Though it can make people uncomfortable, or make them say unflattering things behind your back, you can't let yourself be talked into going along with something when you know it can be better. Ever. To settle for second best is a violation of the rules of Simplicity, and it plants the seeds for disappointment, extra work, and more meetings. Most disturbing, it puts you in the worst possible business position: having to defend an idea you never believed in.

Your challenge is to become unbending when it comes to enforcing your standards. Mercilessly so. If you submit only the work you believe in 100 percent and approve only the work you believe in 100 percent, you own something that no one can take away from you: integrity.

As often happens in life, one must often suffer the consequences of doubting before becoming a believer. I'm not proud of it, but that's the way I learned my lesson about standards.

After a week of hard work by several creative teams, it came time to choose which ads we would present to Steve Jobs the next day. It was that moment when you distill all ideas down to the point where you'd be proud to run any ad on the table. This is when the standards had to be ruthlessly enforced.

Maybe I caught a bug, the dog ate my judgment, or whatever—for some reason my defenses crumbled. One creative team had knocked themselves out on this project and truly, passionately believed in their work. I didn't love what they'd done. But they practically begged me not to cut it out of the presentation, and I let my compassion step between me and my standards. I kept their ads in the show.

When we met with Steve Jobs, I laid the work out in front of him. He pointed right to the suspect ads and said, "Ah. So you put the B team on this one, did you?"

I was busted. The truth is, I thought those ads were "good enough," and I'd included them with another series of ads I thought was much better. But there they sat, diminishing the quality of our show. What I had done was easier, not smarter. Now I'd have to work to gain back the credibility points I'd just lost with Steve. I'd made my life more complicated.

I took Steve's icy words to heart. I knew I'd originally had the right instincts, but I had allowed myself to compromise. Good intentions or bad, the effect was the same. That was enough for me to pledge that I'd never again put myself in a position where I had to defend something I didn't believe in.

In Apple's world, every manager has to be a ruthless enforcer of high standards. If you're willing to alter your standards from situation to situation, you and Simplicity are going to have a rocky relationship. Compromise will often just send you back to the drawing board and raise questions about your own talent in a client's mind.

Brutality with Style

There are plenty of stories out there about evil CEOs who are relentless, demanding, and thoroughly unbearable. One large subset of those stories is found in the folder marked "Jobs, Steve."

Yes, Steve absolutely was relentless and demanding, but we could debate the unbearable part. I personally witnessed quite a few people being verbally assaulted, but only a few who found it harsh enough to quit over. Most people understood that Steve was pushing them for a purpose. They knew that "being Steved" didn't necessarily mean you were marked for death.

One could always find comfort in the fact that Steve did a hard reset from meeting to meeting. If you had a flaming fight with him one day, the next day it would most likely be business as usual. Unless, of course, you went ahead and set him off again in your new meeting. The hard reset ensured that every situation would be dealt with on its merits. Just because you had been a dunce yesterday did not mean that you'd be labeled a dunce today. The way to get back in Steve's good graces was simply to demonstrate your worth.

Anyone who worked with Steve for a substantial period of time has plenty of good stories to share. Some are amusing in their own right, while others are funny at least partly because you weren't on the receiving end of whatever Steve did.

Steve had wit, though, and he often used that to express his disdain for traditional corporate structures. There's a story from the early days of Macintosh back at Chiat/Day, when one of the agency guys eagerly introduced himself to Steve on the set of a shoot.

"What do you do at the agency?" Steve asked.

"I'm an account guy," he replied.

"Oh, so you're overhead," said Steve.

Though it was said in jest, Steve wasn't kidding. He had no problem investing millions in projects he believed in. He had no problem walking away from investments simply because his strategy had shifted. (He once killed one of our TV campaigns on the eve of production for that reason, dumping over a million dollars in the process.) He just had an awful aversion to spending money foolishly or not getting enough in return. He didn't hold high respect for the "handlers," only for the people who did the actual work.

Another good Steve moment came when he interviewed Chiat/Day's candidate to manage his global business. Steve was impressed by those who'd done great work on great accounts, and on paper this person's credentials were unassailable. He was the lead account person on the hottest piece of business at one of the nation's hottest creative agencies. Chiat/Day was confident that his credentials were Steve-proof and shipped the candidate up for an interview.

"So what are you doing now?" Steve asked.

"I'm the global account director on Nike at Wieden & Kennedy," said our man, knowing he was holding a straight flush.

Steve paused. He was a big fan of the Nike brand.

"Nike has been great for a long time," said Steve.

"Thanks," said the candidate.

"So … your job is to not fuck anything up," he concluded.

Steve ended up approving that hire. He just wanted to make sure our man understood the difference between working on an account in serious need of help—like Apple at the time—and maintaining a piece of business where the client is already firing on all cylinders. This was the type of honesty Steve displayed with everyone, whether he was interviewing them or actively working with them.

In fact, I have Steve to thank for what was absolutely the most uncomfortable meeting of my professional life, a meeting that took place back in the days of NeXT. It was a veritable festival of brutal honesty. But to appreciate that meeting, you must first appreciate the events that led up to it.

After building NeXT from scratch over several years, Steve was ready to launch the company's first product, the NeXT Computer. So it was time for us to create the company's first ad campaign. Given the importance Steve placed on advertising and the importance of this moment to the future of NeXT, this presentation was beyond critical.

The NeXT/agency relationship was just forming in those days, so there wouldn't be a whole lot to stop Steve from jumping ship if he suddenly decided we weren't right for the job. Considering we lived and worked three thousand miles away from NeXT, the relationship had plenty of potential for strain.

Because this was an important moment, agency leader Ralph Ammirati had decided to bring in one of his favorite freelance designers to help us develop a distinct design for the NeXT campaign. It would define all of NeXT's marketing materials moving forward. Ralph's choice was a very sweet woman with a long history at Chiat/Day. She had exquisite taste, a wall full of design awards, and a burning desire to give Steve something great. On paper, she sounded perfect.

However, in one of the most stunning misreads in technology advertising history, this designer—with the full support of the agency—recommended that Steve should zag when the others were zigging. She had this brilliant idea that Steve should launch his much-anticipated, super-high-tech company by adopting a distinctly untechy look. She designed a series of long-copy ads in which the text wrapped around a number of images that called out the features of the NeXT Computer. But instead of using modern photography to show off the world's most advanced computer, she decided to adopt a hand-illustrated, black-and-white, woodcut style. That is, the images were decidedly quaint and old-fashioned, more appropriate for the *Farmer's Almanac*.

In the retelling, this of course sounds like a colossal blunder. However, at the time, when the agency was on a quest to do something different, you'd be surprised how many really smart advertising people thought this was a great idea. At NeXT headquarters during that first presentation, Steve was dumbfounded when he looked at the work. He rejected it quickly. That set us up for our meeting the following week, which would turn so very uncomfortable.

We arrived at NeXT headquarters with all-new work and an all-new attitude. Now we had redesigned our ads with a much more modern look, and we were ready to redeem ourselves. Meeting time. But as we started to pull the ads out of our portfolios, Steve said, "Hey, listen, before we look at the new stuff, I want to talk about what happened last week."

His voice was calm. It didn't indicate danger ahead. But as he spoke, that calm voice slowly became more angry and agitated, and then he got madder still, to the point where he talked himself into some major (and loud) verbal abuse. The condensed version went like this: "The work you showed me last week was shit. I knew it was shit, *you* knew it was shit, but you came all the way out here and showed it to me anyway. That's not acceptable and I never want it to happen again. Ever."

Steve definitely deserved points for honesty, but from the agency's point of view, it wasn't exactly the right mood-setter to start off a new presentation designed to win his love. Happily, Steve ended up being enthusiastic about the new ads, and that felt good, even if we could still sort of hear the echo in the room of his earlier attack. This was the campaign that came to be used by NeXT throughout its lifetime: a modern look with thick black headlines and bold photography—clearly cut from the same cloth as the BMW ads that had attracted Steve to the agency in the first place.

So on the work level, we were fine. Credibility restored, the agency was ready to forge ahead into production. But not so fast.

Just as he had at the start of the meeting, Steve felt compelled to have another chat with us. Now relieved over the work, he wanted to pick up on the conversation he'd started with. He told us that he felt a little bad that he had been so angry when we first sat down. He explained that our previous meeting had been weighing on his mind. He'd considered saying nothing and waiting to see the quality of our work in round two, but he thought it was important to clear the air. That's why he'd spoken up.

In his more reflective mood, and having been satisfied by our new thinking, he thought it would be helpful to tell us where we stood, now that we were a few months into our working relationship. He was going to go around the room and grade our performances, one by one. I got the lucky seat—in the last position—so I got to watch the show as Steve dished out his brutal honesty in carefully measured individual doses.

The account manager got an A. Steve was very happy with the way the business side of things was being handled. The media guy got a B-plus. He was competent, but Steve wasn't exactly wowed. Next up was my partner, the art director. Bad news for him: He got an F. Steve was holding him responsible for last week's fiasco, even though it was the secret art director who had actually done the work. "If you can't do a better job than that, you're going to have to replace yourself," said Steve.

Finally it was my turn. I'm pleased to report that I received an A-minus. "You're doing great, but you still have to shake a few of those Chiat/Day cobwebs loose," said Steve.

That assessment was interesting in two ways, covering two different decades. First, Chiat/Day had done some of the most remarkable work that Apple—and the entire ad industry—had ever seen and had played a huge role in the success of the original Macintosh. You'd think that he would have been very interested in having some of those cobwebs around. Second, ten years after this conversation, and with great enthusiasm, Steve would sign up Chiat/Day—cobwebs and all—to be Apple's agency once again when he was reinstalled as Apple's leader.

Our report cards verbally delivered, several fairly happy people and one depressed art director packed up and flew back to New York. We had finally succeeded in giving Steve a campaign he was excited about, and thanks to his honesty, we all knew exactly where we stood with him.

It may not always be welcome news, but there is great value in understanding the state of your relationship—knowing what you've done right, what you've done wrong, and what you must do to ensure a happy future. No matter how unpleasant it might have been at times, we did get that with Steve, and it worked to the benefit of all. It's when things are left unresolved that people spend too much of their time looking over their shoulders instead of looking ahead. That's when Complexity creeps in. In Steve's simplified world, such extraneous issues didn't get much of a chance to distract.

The Rotating Turret

There was a certain amount of theater that went on inside Apple. The rules were well known, and a number of dramas played out with predictability.

That Steve Jobs was intolerant of stupidity is a matter of record. He wasn't at all polite when stupidity reared its ugly head. He especially wasn't fond of employing stupidity, so if you were on Apple's staff and wanted to retain that status, it was wise not to display your lack of smarts in a meeting with him. You'd just set him off and get it right between the eyes.

A former Apple senior staffer remembers a routine that he saw played out often during his time as a direct report to Steve. He calls it "the rotating turret." There was no predicting when it would happen, as it depended on how conversations evolved. But in some meeting, at some random time, some poor soul in the room would say something that everyone in the room could tell was going to light Steve's fuse.

First came the uncomfortable pause.

The offending comment would reverberate in the air, and it would seem as if the entire world went into slow motion as Steve's internal sensors fixed on the origin of the sound wave. You could almost hear the meshing of gears as Steve's "turret" slowly turned toward the guilty party. Everyone knew what was coming—but was powerless to stop it.

Finally, Steve's turret would lock on to its target. In a split second he would activate his firing mechanism, and without a second thought he'd unload all his ammunition. It was uncomfortable to watch and even more uncomfortable to experience, but at Apple it was just a fact of life.

Learn to Take a Punch

With a CEO that unrestrained and determined to let you know where you stand, you'd think the halls of Apple would have been littered with bodies. But mostly it was the senior staff who had to deal directly with Steve, and just because you'd been attacked didn't mean you'd been fired. If you left the room employed, you'd likely find yourself stronger. Now you were a survivor. You'd develop a growing immunity to attacks, frontal and otherwise.

Since emotional breakdowns in the office are never a good idea, having a thicker skin is a decided advantage. I'm proud to say that in over a decade of working directly with Steve, between NeXT and Apple, I was on the receiving end of a scary outburst on only two occasions, both of which will be forever etched into my memory. For one, I literally had to travel 7,500 miles to receive my pummeling in a Hawaiian paradise, just a few palm trees down the trail from the Jobs family vacation hut. The other I took via telephone at my agency desk. You'd think it would be less scary that way, but it wasn't.

While these experiences were jarring at the time, I now wear them as a badge of courage. If you worked in Steve's world, and you didn't have such an experience, you might even feel cheated.

There are hundreds of people who know what it was like to be on the receiving end of a Steve tirade. But what about Steve? How did he hold up to a blistering verbal attack from others? He developed a thick skin early in his career. Back in 1997, when Apple was on its deathbed and Steve was the returning hero to many, one of the first things he did was pull the plug on the Mac clones. The previous regime had licensed other computer makers to sell Mac-compatible desktops. The idea was that this might help open the floodgates to new users and save a platform that was suffering a world of hurt.

Steve hated this idea. He wanted Apple to control the hardware and software, period. Even back then, Steve talked about the need to control the complete experience and never put Apple's customers in a position where they might enjoy the benefits of the Mac OS but suffer the short-comings of non-Apple hardware. However, many in the Apple community had come to embrace the clones and believe that this expansion of the Mac OS was necessary for Apple's survival. When Steve nixed the idea, they crucified him. Many worried that he hadn't learned his lesson out in the wild and was still prone to rash moves that would endanger the company.

I was surprised at the ferocity of the attacks. The naysayers were lashing out at Steve as a professional and as a person. But for Steve it was business as usual. This wasn't the first time he'd been criticized, and he knew it wouldn't be the last. He could easily compartmentalize the incoming news. He absorbed what he wished and blocked out the rest.

I further came to appreciate Steve's thick skin when the TBS network broadcast its original movie *Pirates of Silicon Valley* in 1999. Steve was tickled when the project was announced. He was gushing like a teenager when he learned that his role was going to be played by Noah Wyle, who had gained fame for his role in NBC's popular *ER* series.

A week before the movie aired, Steve told us that he would be hosting a dinner party at home with friends to watch the grand debut. Having spent small fortunes with TBS on behalf of Apple and other clients, the agency had been issued an advance copy earlier in the week. So I invited the creative group to a combination pizza lunch and movie screening. The pizza was fabulous. The movie made us wince. It wasn't exactly a high-quality production. It was also obvious that the story was exaggerated and time-lines twisted for the sake of drama.

Of most concern to us was the fact that Steve was portrayed as such a flawed character. In the movie (and in real life), he had refused to acknowledge paternity of his child or provide so much as a nickel for child support, even though he was by then worth millions. It was not a flattering portrayal. (Note: As most know, Steve ultimately did accept responsibility, becoming close with his daughter and contributing to her support.)

My first thought was, "Hmm, Steve might want to reconsider that little dinner party."

I did my due diligence and told Steve that the movie painted a negative picture, but he was unfazed. He wasn't surprised that the movie would be fictionalized. That's just the way things work.

I next saw Steve on the Monday immediately following the weekend debut of *Pirates*. I wasn't sure if I should even bring it up, but it turned out that I didn't have to. Before our meeting began, Steve asked the whole team if we had seen the movie. He wore a big grin and seemed to be on a high about it. I was wondering if we had seen the same movie. He seemed to buy the notion that any publicity is good publicity, and the negatives just rolled off his back.

Chapter 2
Think Small

Apple encourages big thinking but small everything else. That is, if you feel the urge to speak or act in a manner reminiscent of anything you learned in a big company, it's best that you do that in the privacy of your own home.

Meeting size is a good example. Once Chiat/Day was installed as Apple's agency of record and we'd settled into our work, we would meet with Steve Jobs every other Monday.

Typically there would be no formal agenda. We'd share our work in progress with Steve and he'd share whatever news he had. This was how we all stayed up to date. The invitee list for these meetings was small. On the agency side were the creative people, account director, and media director. On the Apple side were Steve, Phil Schiller (product marketing), Jony Ive (design), Allen Olivo (marketing communications), and Hiroki Asai (Apple's in-house creative). Special guest stars were invited as required.

One particular day, there appeared in our midst a woman from Apple with whom I was unfamiliar. I don't recall her name, as she never appeared in our world again, so for the purposes of this tale, I'll call her Lorrie. She took her seat with the rest of us as Steve breezed into the boardroom, right on time.

Steve was in a sociable mood, so we chatted it up for a few minutes, and then the meeting began. "Before we start, let me just update you on a few things," said Steve, his eyes surveying the room. "First off, let's talk about iMac—"

He stopped cold. His eyes locked on to the one thing in the room that didn't look right. Pointing to Lorrie, he said, "Who are you?"

Lorrie was a bit stunned to be called out like that, but she calmly explained that she'd been asked to attend because she was involved with some of the marketing projects we'd be discussing. Steve heard it. Processed it. Then he hit her with the Simple Stick.

"I don't think we need you in this meeting, Lorrie. Thanks," he said. Then, as if that diversion had never occurred—and as if Lorrie never existed—he continued with his update.

So, just as the meeting started, in front of eight or so people whom Steve *did* want to see at the table, poor Lorrie had to pack up her belongings, rise from her chair, and take the long walk across the room toward the door.

Her crime: She wasn't necessary.

Simplicity's Best Friend: Small Groups of Smart People

What Lorrie experienced was the strict enforcement of one of Simplicity's most important rules: Start with small groups of smart people—and keep them small. Every time the body count goes higher, you're simply inviting Complexity to take a seat at the table.

The small-group principle is deeply woven into the religion of Simplicity. It's key to Apple's ongoing success and key to any organization that wants to nurture quality thinking. The idea is pretty basic: Everyone in the room should be there for a reason. There's no such thing as a "mercy invitation." Either you're critical to the meeting or you're not. It's nothing personal, just business.

Steve Jobs actively resisted any behavior he believed representative of the way big companies think—even though Apple had been a big company for many years. He knew that small groups composed of the smartest and most creative people had propelled Apple to its amazing success, and he had no intention of ever changing that. When he called a meeting or reported to a meeting, his expectation was that everyone in the room would be an essential participant. Spectators were not welcome.

This was based on the somewhat obvious idea that a smaller group would be more focused and motivated than a large group, and smarter people will do higher quality work.

For a principle that would seem to be Common Sense, it's surprising how many organizations fail to observe it. How many overpopulated meetings do you sit through during the course of a year? How many of those meetings get sidetracked or lose focus in a way that would never occur if the group were half the size? The small-group rule requires enforcement, but it's worth the cost.

Remember, Complexity normally offers the easy way out. It's easier to remain silent and let the Lorries of the world take their seats at the table, and most of us are too mannerly to perform a public ejection. But if you don't act to keep the group small, you're creating an exception to the rule— and Simplicity is never achieved through exceptions. Truthfully, you can do the brutal thing without being brutal. Just explain your reasons. Keep the group small.

Prior to working with Steve Jobs, I worked with a number of more traditional big companies. So it was a shock to my system (in a good way) when I entered Steve's world of Simplicity. In Apple's culture, progress was much easier to attain. It was also a shock to my system (in a bad way) when I left Steve's world and found myself suffering through the same old issues with more traditional organizations again.

Back in the early days of NeXT, when all of its promise lay ahead, I heard Steve address the troops one day, telling them to savor this moment in time. He told them that when NeXT got bigger and more successful, they'd fondly look back at this time as "the good old days." Things would surely get crazier. (Not the most accurate of his predictions, given NeXT's constant struggles, but you get the point.) In later years, when I found myself attending larger, less productive meetings at multilayered companies, those words would echo in my head. I did miss the good old days—not just because they were quieter but because they were smarter.

Out in the real world, when I talk about small groups of smart people, I rarely get any pushback. That's because Common Sense tells us it's the right way to go. Most people know from experience that the fastest way to lose focus, squander valuable time, and water down great ideas is to entrust them to a larger group. Just as we know that there is equal danger in putting ideas at the mercy of a large group of approvers.

One reason why large, unwieldy groups tend to be created in many companies is that the culture of a company is bigger than any one person. It's hard to change "the way we do things here." This is where the zealots of Simplicity need to step in and overcome the inertia.

One must be judicious and realistic about applying the small-group principle. Simply making groups smaller will obviously not solve all problems, and "small" is a relative term. Only you know your business and the nature of your projects, so only you can draw the line between too few people and too many. You need to be the enforcer and be prepared to hit the process with the Simple Stick when the group is threatened with unnecessary expansion.

Over the years, Apple's marketing group has fine-tuned a process that's been successfully repeated, revolution by revolution. Project teams are kept small, with talented people being given real responsibility—which is what drives them to work some crazy hours and deliver quality thinking. Because quality is stressed over quantity, meetings are informal and visible progress is made on a weekly (if not daily) basis.

Every company wants to maximize productivity and cut down on unnecessary meetings. How they go about it, though, can vary widely. At Apple, forming small groups of smart people comes naturally, because in its culture, that's "the way we do things here." Sometimes companies try to "legislate" productivity by offering up corporate guidelines.

In one iconic technology company with which I worked, I found a framed sign in every conference room designed to nudge the employees toward greater productivity. The headline on the sign was HOW TO HAVE A SUCCESSFUL MEETING. The content read like it came right out of a corporate manual, which it likely did. It featured a bullet-pointed list of things like "State the agenda at the start of your meeting," "Encourage participation by all attendees," and "Conclude your meeting with agreement on next steps."

What these signs really said, though, was "Welcome to a very big company! Just follow these signs and you'll fit in well." It's not hard to imagine Steve Jobs, who actively fought big-company behavior, gleefully ripping these signs off the wall and replacing them with Ansel Adams prints that might provide a moment of reflection or inspiration—like those he put up in the halls of NeXT.

If you have any thought of working at Apple, I'm sorry to say there will be no signs on the wall telling you how to run a meeting. Likewise, there will be no signs telling you how to tie your shoes or fill a glass of water. The assumption made at your hiring is that you are well equipped with Brains and Common Sense and that you're a fully functioning adult. If you're not already a disciple of Simplicity, you'll become one soon. Either that or you'll decide you'd rather not be part of such a thing, which is okay too. Simplicity prefers not having to train a bucking bronco.

If big companies really feel compelled to put something on their walls, a better sign might read:

How to Have a Great Meeting

1. Throw out the least necessary person at the table.
2. Walk out of this meeting if it lasts more than 30 minutes.
3. Do something productive today to make up for the time you spent here.

I'm exaggerating, of course. Meetings are a necessary and important way to make collaborative progress. But we all know that too many unnecessary or overpopulated meetings can rob even the most brilliant people of their creative energy.

More than being a guideline for meetings, however, the small-group principle is mandatory for project groups.

Many businesses follow an instinctive but misguided principle: The more critical the project, the more people must be thrown at it. The operative theory is that more brains equal more ideas. That's hard to argue with—except that only occasionally do more brains mean *better* ideas.

The more people involved in the effort, the more complicated briefings become, the more hand-holding is required to get people up to speed, and the more time must be spent reviewing participants' work and offering useful feedback. A smaller group offers the most efficient way to succeed—assuming that it also has the smarts. (Promise you'll never forget that part.)

To say that putting more people on a project will improve the results is basically saying that you don't have a ton of confidence in the group you started with. Either that or you're just looking for an insurance policy—which *also* means you don't have a lot of confidence in the group you started with. Whatever your motivation, what you're really saying is that you don't have the right people on the job. So fix that. When populated by the smartest people, small groups will give management more confidence, not less.

When you push for small groups of smart people, everybody wins. The company gets better thinking. The group feels better appreciated and is eager to take on more work. This type of organization actually fuels productivity, project to project.

Apple's agency, originally known as Chiat/Day, succeeded by the same philosophy. Led by the Hall of Fame creative director Lee Clow, our small group matched up well with Apple's small group. Limiting the size of our group helped us produce work quickly, get information fast, and have the agility to react to unexpected events.

The agency's founder, the late Jay Chiat, had set a similar tone decades earlier. Jay and Steve had a unique relationship in the days of the original

Macintosh and in certain ways were cut from the same cloth. I had the pleasure of being personally ejected from a meeting by Jay during one of my several stints at Chiat/Day. It happened much like Steve's ejection of Lorrie, except that I was only half of a dual ejection. Surveying the room before the start of a meeting, Jay took one look at my art director partner and me and said, "What are you guys doing here?"

"Beats me," I said. "We're just responding to the invitation."

"You shouldn't be sitting around a table talking about this bullshit," said Jay. "Go create something." At least we got to walk out of the room with smiles on our faces. Lorrie didn't have that option.

The working styles of both Jay and Steve have stuck with me over the years. I can think of no better examples of leaders with a talent for keeping their teams focused on the mission and focused on producing great results. And both built spectacularly successful businesses. It's not a coincidence.

To this day I have a recurring fantasy when I find myself trapped in a big meeting going nowhere. I imagine what Steve Jobs would say and do if he were sitting in that room, enduring what I'm enduring. In my fantasy, it's like having a really good seat for a matinee at the Roman Colosseum. Who would Steve verbally dismantle or eject from the meeting? When would he cut the presenter off midsentence and say it's all bullshit? With all the talk about how rough Steve could be, it should be acknowledged that oftentimes he was only doing what many of us wish we could do. Steve saw no reason to be delicate when his time, and the time of everyone in the room, was being wasted.

This is part of the challenge that we non-Steves must face. Most of us aren't comfortable with the idea of turning into coldhearted control freaks, but we also know that we sometimes need to be tough to keep projects on track.

The good news is, being brutal and being respected are not mutually exclusive. In fact, showing a little of that brutal honesty at the right time is a pretty good way to earn respect—and keep those smart groups small.

Think Big, Act Small

Speaking at the All Things Digital conference in 2010, Steve Jobs revealed a bit about Apple's inner workings:

> *You know how many committees we have at Apple? Zero. We're organized like a start-up. We're the biggest start-up on the planet.*

Steve's devotion to Simplicity was such that he couldn't tolerate a complicated hierarchy. To the core of his being, he believed he could lead a global company to success without falling into the evil clutches of Complexity. More specifically, he believed the new Apple could succeed by remaining true to the values of the old Apple. As he put it:

> *I don't see why you have to change as you get big.*

It sounds unrealistic. After all, how can a company *not* change as it gets bigger, as it scales from serving thousands to serving tens of millions? But Steve rarely believed that something couldn't be done, so he just did what he thought was right—which included enforcing the small-company mentality. He was driven by a sense of idealism, of how things should really work, even when that flew in the face of traditional corporate behavior.

John Sculley, the oft-vilified CEO who engineered Steve's ouster from Apple in 1985, explained Steve's organizational principles in a 2010 interview:

> *Steve had a rule that there could never be more than one hundred people on the Mac team. So if you wanted to add someone, you had to take someone out. And the thinking was a typical Steve Jobs observation: "I can't remember more than a hundred first names, so I only want to be around people that I know personally. So if it gets bigger than a hundred people, it will force us to go to a different organization structure where I can't work that way. The way I like to work is where I touch everything."*

Through the whole time I knew him at Apple that's exactly how he ran his division.

This changed little from the time Apple was launching Macintosh to Steve's last days at work. One of the things Steve institutionalized was an annual off-site meeting of Apple's global executives called the Top 100. These were the people he trusted to understand Apple's vision and make sure it was absorbed by their direct reports. At the Top 100 meeting, Steve and his executive team would lay out the strategies for the coming year and provide a glimpse into the years beyond. It's a safe bet that Steve knew the Top 100 by their first names.

Back in the garage, when Apple Computer, Inc., was born, Jobs, Wozniak, and associates formed the ultimate small group of smart people. It was Apple's smaller, entrepreneurial roots that made Steve a believer in this way of working. What's astounding is that it didn't just fuel Apple's growth in becoming a larger company—it fueled enough growth to make Apple the most valuable company on the planet. (Or the second-most-valuable, depending on how Apple's stock price matches up with ExxonMobil's on any given day.)

The Laws of Small

Let's assume that you've got the "smart" half of "small groups of smart people" taken care of. (Congratulations on that.) Let's concentrate for a moment on the "small" part. During my speckled career in advertising, I've succeeded in reducing it to the following scientific principle:

> **The quality of work resulting from a project is inversely proportional to the number of people involved in the project.**

In other words, the more people you put in a room, the lower your chances of getting anything good out of it. However, the concern about the makeup of a group isn't entirely about crowd control. There's one particular person whose involvement in the group is critical. In fact, this point is so important, it deserves its very own principle:

The quality of work resulting from a project increases in direct proportion to the degree of involvement by the ultimate decision maker.

That ultimate decision maker doesn't have to be the CEO. It could be whichever manager has been given responsibility. But somebody has decision-making authority, and the involvement of that person has to be part of the deal. It's counterproductive—and frustrating as hell—for any group to work on a project for weeks or months before getting feedback on their direction from the responsible authority. This person needs to be involved in the briefing and remain as engaged as possible at points throughout the process.

At most large companies, you'll be told it's unrealistic for a chief executive to become too involved in marketing. That's why it was good to have an unrealistic guy like Steve Jobs around. He was no less enthusiastic about being involved in a marketing meeting than he was about being involved in a product design meeting. He understood that both were vital to Apple's success. He knew that if he participated in the marketing process, directing a small group of smart people, Apple would continue to market circles around its competitors.

Steve didn't believe in delegating significant marketing decisions to others. He was there for every presentation and stayed current with every project's progress. During the *Think different* years, I can personally attest that he was involved with every image and every word. Not tyrannically so, but as an eager participant. I lost track of the number of midnight phone calls we had just to go over the copy for an ad about to be published.

Steve enforced one policy I've never seen implemented anywhere else. I wouldn't be surprised if he was the only big-company CEO on earth who worked this way. He wouldn't allow anyone to see the agency's creative ideas before he did. He didn't want anyone, even the VP of marketing, to filter the work before he had a chance to view it. "I don't want someone guessing what I'm going to like or not like," Steve explained on more than one occasion. "Maybe I'll see a spark in there that nobody else sees."

Most CEOs clearly don't share Steve's passion for marketing. Many, justifiably, would say they simply don't have that kind of time. That's what makes it all the more remarkable that Steve somehow found the time when he was working as CEO of both Apple and Pixar. The bottom line is this: If you think it's important, you find time for it. If you're really that busy, or if marketing isn't one of your major skills, you need to hire/delegate someone to do the job—and give them real authority.

Small Groups = Better Relationships

Given the well-documented mood swings of Steve Jobs, you'd think that the relationship between Apple and its agency would have frequently been stressed to the breaking point. Stressed, yes. To the breaking point, no. On the contrary, Steve and Chiat/Day had one of the longest-running, most successful partnerships in marketing history.

The reason? Surprise. It was small groups of smart people. That's what enabled Chiat/Day to keep the tight relationship going with Steve Jobs and Apple. That's what has allowed it to keep doing great work. And that's what has allowed it to keep the relationship going when things get tense. In many ways, these types of relationships are like a marriage, and a good marriage finds a way to survive.

Chiat/Day worked with Apple for five years beginning in 1980; the two reunited in 1997, and they continue to work together to this day. That's an unusually long partnership by ad industry norms. Chiat/Day chief Lee Clow and Steve Jobs forged a close relationship back when the original Macintosh was launched, and it surprised few when Steve moved his business back to Chiat/Day upon his return to Apple in 1997. By this time, the agency had merged its way into becoming TBWA\Chiat\Day. (From this point on, I'll drop the formality and simply refer to the agency as "Chiat," as most people do. Which also avoids the use of those silly backslashes.)

Interestingly, when Chiat was pitching the IBM PC business during the days when Apple had moved its advertising business to agency BBDO, one of IBM's biggest concerns about Chiat was its reputation for burning through clients quickly. IBM had its heart set on finding long-lasting love. As fate would have it, Apple would not only return to Chiat but would stick with the agency much longer than IBM would stick with making PCs.

Small groups of smart people are an important part of the cultures on both sides of the Chiat-Apple equation. Both organizations are set up that way internally, and the two small groups mesh well when they meet.

True, there were moments when Steve would threaten to fire the agency, but there were other moments when he would tell us, almost misty-eyed, how much he appreciated something we had done. Most important was that at the end of the day, both sides knew where they stood. They had a shared passion. They also had honesty—brutal at times, but mostly just the good old-fashioned, don't-hide-anything-from-your-partner kind of honesty. When problems arose, they were fixed quickly. Apple's relationship with Chiat had deep roots, and that gave both sides a sense of security and responsibility.

If I needed proof that the relationship between Apple and Chiat was special, I would find it the moment I left that job to start working on the Intel account at the agency Euro NY.

Way back before Euro ever took over the business, Intel was known as a "difficult" client. This, of course, was a polite description used by those currently *in* the relationship. Former colleagues who had worked with Intel in the past used words that were considerably less polite.

Unlike Apple, Intel was a big company that acted like a big company. Whereas at Apple there was nothing more important than the work, at Intel that wasn't quite so obvious. There were often side issues, overanalyses, second-guessing, any number of things that tended to distract from the task of creating something great. There was both friction and formality in the agency-client relationship that stemmed from two large groups of people working together.

Certain strains in the relationship were evident. To improve our interactions, every quarter Intel would do for us what any loving partner would do for his or her soul mate: provide a "report card" noting the highlights and lowlights of our relationship, detailing what deficiencies needed to be corrected. It also asked for a report card in return, which we dutifully delivered. This was a striking difference between the way these large groups worked and the way Apple's small groups worked. It would never have entered Steve's mind to spend valuable time creating and processing report cards. He preferred real-time honesty. If something was bothering him, he'd simply tell us. That was our report card.

The large group at Euro was organized to mirror the hierarchy of the large group of Intel's marketing team. To keep things orderly, there was a more formal atmosphere. Meetings with our Intel clients were more staged and choreographed than were the meetings we had at Apple, which were almost free-form in comparison.

I could write for weeks about the differences between the productivity of small groups in the Chiat-Apple relationship and that of the large groups in the Euro-Intel relationship. But one incident sums it up better than I ever could.

In response to a legal issue that had developed in relation to our advertising, Intel's VP of marketing had asked for the agency's opinion on a course of action. Meeting internally, the team was unanimous in its recommendation. When I sent this opinion to the agency account director and suggested that we send it to the client immediately, I received an email back that started with this classic line:

We can't have an opinion until we know what Intel's opinion is.

That type of attitude perfectly captures the difficulty of dealing with large groups when an account worth millions of dollars is at stake. If you're not careful, honesty can be replaced by calculation and relationships can get "managed" rather than nurtured. Needless to say, if Chiat ever exhibited this type of behavior with Steve Jobs, it wouldn't have a long-standing relationship to celebrate. Ultimately, Intel wasn't all that happy either, as it moved its business to another agency not long after that.

It's Simplicity that keeps Apple's relationship with Chiat solid. It creates a feeling of true partnership, with each party having a stake in the other's success. Small groups of smart people create a tighter relationship that can withstand the test of time, promoting a feeling of common cause and common values.

Getting Smaller by Streamlining

Between Apple and its agency there exists a mountain of creativity. However, these two organizations do not have a monopoly on fresh, exciting, motivating ideas. There are countless smart companies out there, many of them served by bright agencies, which in turn are populated by some terrific creative thinkers.

So why is it that only a small handful of companies are able to produce truly great marketing campaigns? Why is the marketing landscape mostly filled with drivel?

One major reason is that most big organizations are simply awful at thinking small. They're unable to streamline complicated processes. Even when they successfully identify their challenges, develop strategies, and create great work that brings them to life, their processes choke the life out of that work. They inflict endless meetings and multiple approvals upon what should be a simpler way of working.

Intel is an interesting example. In sheer brainpower, Intel is probably the most amazing company on the planet. What it does is almost beyond the ability of mere mortals to comprehend. As it was once described to me by an Intel executive, the investment and effort required to design a processor, build fabrication plants, and mass-produce it is akin to that which went into building NASA's entire fleet of space shuttles. Intel is capable of producing things other companies can't even imagine.

That said, its ads have been mostly pathetic.

Why? Let's blame it on their upbringing. Intel is a company of engineers. They make decisions based on cold, hard, scientific evidence—even when they're making decisions about something that has an emotional component, like marketing. Paul Otellini, Intel's CEO, made that abundantly clear at an internal marketing event where he addressed the entire global team. "At Intel, we make zero-defect products," he said. "What I want to see from this group is zero-defect advertising."

When he spoke those words, a great pain was felt among the creative thinkers in the room. They knew that even the world's greatest film directors couldn't function under the mandate of producing zero-defect movies. Great ideas travel with a degree of risk. There's bound to be a "defect" or two, which, hopefully, will be more than compensated for by the brilliance of the idea. But Otellini's admonition perfectly captured the mind-set of Intel. It encouraged those responsible to redouble their efforts to make sure all processes were in place, and maybe even dream up some new ones if they might help guarantee that zero-defect advertising. In the hyperefficient world of Intel, risk is a defect.

Unfortunately, battening down the hatches is not the best way to help Simplicity thrive. It's finding ways to make a big company work more like a small company that makes things simpler. That involves taking a look at the processes that are in place and figuring out how to reduce them—not reinforce them.

What's ironic is that within Intel (and most every company with which I've worked), people never stop using Apple as an example for some improvement they'd like to make to their own methods. They optimistically believe they can fix their problems by emulating at least one small part of Apple's bigger package.

Unfortunately, this rarely works. Remember, Simplicity is an all-or-none proposition. No picking and choosing allowed. If you can only muster up the energy to buy into part of it, you're just going to hurt yourself trying.

Love of Process vs. Love of Simplicity

It's always interesting to think back to your first meeting with a new client. I'm not talking about all the meetings you had during the courtship; I'm talking about that very first meeting after you officially got hitched.

With some clients, you can look back at that meeting and realize what a perfect indicator it was of things to come. With others, you might realize that you either failed to notice the signs that were there or just totally misread them.

My first meeting with Apple after Steve's return in 1997 beautifully foretold the way things would go in the years ahead. It was fun, interesting, hopeful, energizing, all those things I had hoped it would be. It was completely unstructured, yet we made a ton of progress. I had already put in many years with Steve before that, but this was my first time seeing him as part of a new team. He was no pushover, but he responded well to our work.

My first meetings with Dell and Intel were also accurate indicators. The best word to describe them would be "sobering." That's too bad, because like everyone else in marketing, I walk into my first meetings with the highest of hopes, determined to see the good and to revel in the potential. But with both of these clients, we could tell that process was going to take precedence over creativity. That was unfortunate, because in Apple's world we made great gains, often spontaneously, because the idea always had the highest priority.

For example, we might be midproduction for an ad that had been approved by Steve Jobs, but then we'd have a better idea while filming or editing. There was no problem going back to Steve with the new idea. In fact, he came to expect us to behave that way, and he looked forward to meetings when new ads were on the agenda. Chances were good that he'd agree with our new direction, and even if he didn't, he'd be happy that we cared enough to try (and happy to shoot down our new idea mercilessly on occasion, but that was just Steve).

By contrast, this kind of spontaneity didn't exist in Intel's world. Once the ad had been socialized among various stakeholders, the concept thoroughly researched, revised, and approved, expectations were set. The process didn't allow for substantial change—no matter how big an improvement it might have been. All must bow to the process.

Apple doesn't deal in absolutes like this. A better idea is a better idea. To even speak of putting process before creativity would put one at risk of excommunication from the Church of Simplicity. The high value placed on ideas is one of the things that Steve burned into the Apple culture and it will likely continue to guide the company into the future.

Having also worked for Apple's agency when John Sculley was the CEO, I can testify to the fact that the Sculley-led Apple, at least in the marketing realm, had become almost as process driven as other big companies. The difference between working in Sculley's agency and working in Steve's agency was like night and day.

Steve understood and appreciated the creative process—which, in certain ways, is the relative absence of process. His experience with Apple, Pixar, and Disney gave him a perspective many CEOs will never have. He got how ideas needed to be nurtured and protected. He knew that machinelike analysis would not magically yield creative brilliance. He knew that if he enabled small groups of smart people, good things would happen—even if those results weren't entirely predictable.

There are many who believe Steve Jobs was a creative genius. I think it would be more accurate to say he was a genius who loved creativity. I saw Steve volunteer some great ideas and I saw him suggest some clunkers (which, obviously, we all do at times). But I've never seen a CEO who had Steve's passion for creativity.

Within the walls of Pixar Steve was actually asked to refrain from attending creative meetings, lest a full-scale mutiny break out among the writers and artists. His leadership and vision were much appreciated, his moviemaking talent not so much.

But this is encouraging news for everyone. Steve was proof that you don't need a killer creative skill to change the world through creative thinking. You can build an organization that recognizes the needs of creativity. You can be a steward of creative thinking and become its greatest advocate. You can become skilled in recognizing when a process is more likely to kill a good idea than it is to promote it.

Steve was a brilliant cultivator of creativity. He was truly great at identifying, hiring, and retaining talent and constructing an environment in which magical things would be more likely to happen. That he had a love of art and design was a major plus. Most important, Steve was a sworn enemy of idea-killing processes. It was to nurture and protect great ideas that he insisted on keeping Apple's processes small.

Companies that don't have a leader with Steve's passion tend to see marketing in more clinical terms. For them, marketing is just another spoke in the wheel, an organization within the organization. Chief marketers in these companies typically demand brilliant creativity but support processes that make it difficult. They seem to think that if they demand greatness, it will somehow land on their desk. They tend to envision a beautiful machine where briefings go in one end and great creative work comes out the other. Unfortunately, great ideas are usually messier than that.

During my first week on a major technology account, I had dinner with my new client, the VP of marketing. She was a big fan of the work Chiat had done on behalf of Apple and was eager to find out whatever she could about how she might improve her company's processes to achieve that kind of quality.

"I won't ask you to betray any secrets," she said, "but I'd love to just ask in general terms if there's anything special that Apple does to produce so much great work so consistently."

I told her that one of the most important things Apple does is trust itself. During my time at Chiat, we didn't test a single ad. Not for print, TV, billboards, the web, retail, or anything.

"Really," she said. "No testing at all. That's interesting." Clearly this was a surprise, so she thought about it for a moment, then continued, "Well, that's something we can't do. Is there anything else you can share?"

This is the problem that most big companies face. Their processes have become so institutionalized, they're incapable of altering their own behavior—even if the benefits of change are staring them right in the face.

It boils down to this: When process is king, ideas will never be. It takes only Common Sense to recognize that the more layers you add to a process, the more watered down the final work will become.

Simplicity Is the Ultimate Efficiency

Working with the marketing group at Intel, I could understand the reasons for the complexities in its operations. It was part of the never-ending quest for efficiency. Efficiency is good, right?

Well, yes and no. Efficiency is a wonderful thing when you're etching millions of microscopic transistors into a silicon wafer. But brilliant marketing plans—and brilliant ads—aren't created by machinery. They're the result of many subjective, nontechnology decisions made by people who (hopefully) have insights about human behavior. Dialing up an emotional connection to customers isn't quite the same as programming a robot on the assembly line.

Apple is an exceptional company in that it is ruthless about operating efficiently (thank you, Tim Cook), yet it never loses sight of its humanity. Its connection to people is essential to its business.

Intel is a company that was founded on engineering excellence, so it is also ruthless about efficiency. But its product—microprocessors—isn't quite as warm and fuzzy as an iPad. So Intel's obsession with efficiency pervades every part of the company—including marketing.

While Apple was willing to put ads on the air based largely on instinct, Intel required cold, hard, convincing scientific proof.

Organizationally, the difference was that Apple took the "small" approach, trusting its marketing fate to a small group of smart people. Intel went big, involving people and processes around the world.

Ironically, it was Intel's quest for efficiency that made its marketing process so inefficient. It would take far more time than Apple, and spend far more money, just to ensure that its product was absolutely perfect. Only one problem with that approach: It didn't work.

As proof, I direct your attention to the last fifteen years' worth of Intel ads. While at select points along the way Intel has managed to produce some interesting moments—such as the initial "Sponsors of Tomorrow" campaign created by the agency Venables Bell & Partners in San Francisco—for the most part its quest for efficiency has produced results that range from embarrassing to forgettable.

Its laptop processor campaign in 2005 that offered better "experiences in your lap" was funny in unintended ways, featuring various celebrities sitting on people's laps. Another series of ads featured singing processors about to leave the factory. That ruthless efficiency clearly didn't prevent the duds from reaching the air.

Over the same period of time, Apple churned out one award-winning campaign after the next. And it didn't waste a minute or a cent on scientific analysis before it sent them out into the world.

And herein lies one of Simplicity's most powerful selling points. Though some companies will literally spend millions of dollars in the name of efficiency, the truth is that Simplicity is the ultimate efficiency.

Assuming that your organization has the talent, respecting the rules of Simplicity results in lower costs, faster work, better work—and, most important, more effective work.

Keeping Hierarchy at Bay

I'd like to say that when you work in an organization that believes in Simplicity, life is easier, you work fewer hours, and you return to your loved ones each night perfectly stress free. But I won't.

The truth is, measured by sheer hours of hard work, there's probably zero difference between working with Apple and working with a company like IBM. Work is hard. That's why they call it work. Simplicity can be many things, but it's not your ticket to a life of leisure.

However, measured by the frame of mind in which you do your work—and the frame of mind in which you leave your work—the difference is night and day. In the world of Apple, most people at least wake up each day with a good sense of what needs to be done and why. In more complicated environments, it can be a challenge to decode different points of view and negotiate a labyrinth of approvals that can span weeks or months.

Hierarchies are not only mentally exhausting for those who have to deal with them, but they tend to whittle away the quality of the work as it's shuttled from meeting to meeting.

My experience with Apple was that the organization was refreshingly flat, especially compared with other large technology companies. At the highest level, dealing with Steve, it was extremely flat. As in, "Does Steve like it or not?" But even on projects at a lower level, the hierarchy had a welcome sanity to it. One basically dealt with the same people week to week, and if there was a VP or other executive involved, he or she would appear at regular checkpoints.

If we had new ideas to share at one of our regular meetings with Steve, we'd get instant reactions and our next steps would be clear. If there were changes to be made, we'd normally understand the reason why.

No matter what might change between our Steve meetings—market conditions, current events, or Steve's own evolving opinions—we were living within a process that was easy to follow. It was an ongoing dialogue with a small group of smart people. And it's not like Steve was a stranger between meetings. He was a full, functioning member of our little band who would call or email whenever he had something to say. In other words, he was a rare CEO.

Working with Intel, the agency followed the traditional routine of presentation and discussion, followed by revision. What made it so different from working with Apple was that getting through one meeting normally only meant that you were cleared to present to a higher-up in another meeting. And that person wouldn't necessarily have been privy to the discussions that had gone on at the first meeting. Messy. In these types of organizations, the lower-level people tend to demand a greater quantity of work, just to be sure that somewhere in that giant pile of ideas their bosses will see something they like, and that will reflect well upon them. They're less willing to support positions that don't align perfectly with their marching orders, even if they represent a smarter path.

In multilayered organizations, it's difficult to stand up for imaginative thinking—because it puts your neck on the line. In Apple's flatter organization, it's easier to "think different."

Chapter 3
Think Minimal

All it takes to appreciate Apple's ability to minimize is one good trip to your local Apple Store. The shopping space has been pared down to its essentials, as have the products you buy there. Apple removes the extraneous.

There is no secret as to why. Steve Jobs often spoke publicly about the purity of Apple's thinking. It focuses on one thing and doesn't get distracted by anything else.

One day, back before Mac OS X, I observed an interesting test of that philosophy. It began when Steve Jobs's assistant called with an unusual meeting invitation. Steve wanted Lee Clow and me to attend a special briefing at Apple, unrelated to our regular marketing meetings. Our attendance was mandatory. All we knew was that we'd be getting together with Steve and his senior software team.

When the day arrived, we found ourselves in the Apple boardroom with a cast of characters we'd never met with before. There was Steve, Avie Tevanian (then senior VP of software), and several more of those responsible for Apple software. We still didn't have a clue what this meeting was about, but we were certainly intrigued.

The topic on the table turned out to be Mac OS 9, which at this point was still a few months off. Steve had a fondness for marketing new versions of the Mac operating system, and with each new release we strategized about ways to get more people to upgrade. One reason he was so eager to sell more was that there was so much profit potential in software. "This is how Microsoft does it," Steve said on more than one occasion. "It's like printing money."

He was referring to the fact that once you were past the development phase, building a software "product" was far simpler—and far less costly—than building a computer. "Printing money" was an apt analogy.

The reason for this meeting was that Steve was considering a radically new approach to the next Mac OS update. Rather than charge the normal upgrade price, which in those days was $99, he was thinking of shipping a second version of Mac OS 9 that would be given away for free—but would be supported instead by advertising. The theory was that this would pull in a ton of people who didn't normally upgrade because of the price, but Apple would still generate income through the advertising. And any time an owner of the free version wanted to get rid of the advertising, he or she could simply pay for the ad-free version. Steve's team had worked out the preliminary numbers and the concept seemed financially sound.

It was a shockingly new idea for Lee and me, but the software people in the room had obviously been wrestling with it for a while. Steve provided some details about how the advertising would work. At system start-up, the user would see a sixty-second commercial. This ad could be regularly changed via updates from Apple's servers. Throughout the rest of the OS, ads would appear in places where they had the most relevance. For example, if the print dialogue box indicated that you were running low on printer ink, you might see an ad from Epson with a link to its store—so you could buy some ink right then and there.

The mood in the room seemed to be very positive, and Steve seemed quite intrigued by the idea. In talking about the commercial that would run at start-up, the consensus was that we would invite only premium companies, and they'd be obligated to deliver very high-quality ads. Lee Clow started imagining the kinds of advertisers we might be able to pull in, like Nike and BMW. Many heads in the room nodded in agreement.

Personally, I thought it would be way out of character for Apple to do this. I couldn't help but think of all the times Steve had so proudly shown off the perfect designs of various Apple products, taking care to point out how they'd been whittled down to their essence. The idea of inviting advertising into the simple, clean environment of Mac OS 9 seemed to fly in the face of all of that.

When we left the meeting, Lee and I had the impression this was really going to happen. But thankfully, it did not. It appeared that too many negatives had come up and Steve scrapped the idea as a result.

Though it was odd that Steve had initially been tempted by this approach, it was reassuring that his love of Simplicity had prevailed in the end. Years before this incident, at the 1997 Apple Worldwide Developers Conference, Steve foretold this moment perfectly:

> *People think focus means saying yes to the thing you've got to focus on. But that's not what it means at all. It means saying no to the hundred other good ideas that there are. You have to pick carefully. I'm actually as proud of the things we haven't done as the things we have done. Innovation is saying no to a thousand things.*

I'm sure a lot of people are happy that Steve ultimately said no to this idea.

The Reduction Act of 1998

When Steve Jobs returned to Apple from his eleven-year exile, the company was in a most precarious place. To say it was near death would be to paint too rosy a picture. It was not only near death—it was also being pummeled by critics and abandoned by its own fans.

The company was in this sorry state due to the performance of three previous CEOs, each of whom had committed two unforgivable crimes:

1. They weren't Steve Jobs.
2. They failed to leverage what was truly special about Apple.

Under the leadership of John Sculley, Mike Spindler, and Gil Amelio, Apple continued to lose its magic—and, along with it, market share. It had practically turned into a game for journalists, who would regularly predict what dire fate was in store for the once-great company. For most, Apple's story was only missing a last line. Vital signs were fading.

The sad joke in Apple circles was that the name of the company had ceased to exist in the press without the word "beleaguered" in front of it. The company that had virtually invented the personal computer had failed to blunt the rise of Microsoft-powered PCs. A dark cloud hung over the kingdom.

Ironically, it was failed CEO Gil Amelio who both saved Apple and ultimately cost himself a job. In order to gain a viable next-generation operating system for Macintosh computers, Amelio acquired Steve Jobs's company, NeXT, bringing Steve back to Apple as his personal adviser.

Poor Gil. He failed to notice the asp in the basket.

Steve was working the board behind the scenes, and it became obvious that only he had the vision and charisma to restore the company to greatness. He was the essence of Apple, and the company had never filled the void after he left. The Apple board relieved Gil of his CEO duties and installed Steve as the interim CEO.

Steve didn't have time to relish the moment. He stepped into the role and started making serious changes to Apple's structure and direction. He started getting rid of the bozos (of which there were many), bringing in the bold and brilliant, restructuring the company, and reinspiring those on whose genius Apple would depend. The adventures of Steve were always fun to watch, but it was a great unknown whether anyone—Steve included—could really save Apple.

Remember, Steve had been driven out of Apple for a reason. He had been spending the company into oblivion. And the business he created while in exile—NeXT—wasn't exactly the poster child for profitability. What Steve was about to prove, however, was that by minimizing in the right places, he could focus Apple on doing the things that would restore the company to health.

Steve inherited a line of products that was way too complicated— especially for a company the size of Apple. Management's attempts to please everyone had resulted in a bewildering choice of computer models, including Quadra, Performa, Macintosh LC, PowerBook, and Power Macintosh. The company's offerings were beige and boring, and having to support so many different models was splintering the company's resources, from research and development to marketing. Worst of all, the sheer number of choices was creating confusion for Apple's customers and employees alike. It was bad business all the way around.

At a special event held at Cupertino's Flint Center for the Performing Arts in May 1998, Steve took the stage to make two announcements that would have a profound impact on the future of Apple. The one most remembered is the unveiling of iMac. But his other announcement is the one that created a fundamentally new direction for the company. It wasn't a computer at all—it was a simple chart. A square containing four quadrants. What it represented was Apple's new product strategy.

Basically, Steve hit Apple's entire product line with the Simple Stick. He was going to transition Apple from its multitude of computer models to a simple grid of four: laptops for consumers and pros, and desktops for consumers and pros. It was one of the most dramatic minimizations of a product line in technology history.

Steve's simple graphic was both an example of Simplicity and a corporate road map. This chart made it clear to every Apple employee where the company was going. With one simple image, Steve moved Apple from a truckload of models to a handful. He set the company off on a wild spree of invention, providing inspiration for the engineers and expectations for the customers. And he saved the company the millions of dollars it was spending to support so many models.

Of course, Apple has grown by many orders of magnitude since that day, and its product line has expanded in the process. Note that I say "expanded," not "become more complicated." Apple's product line, which now includes such consumer devices as iPod, iPhone, and iPad, remains a universe away from the urban sprawl of overlapping models being hawked by the PC companies. Every product on Apple's grid has a distinct reason for being that is easily understood by its customers. And every product Apple sells is first quality. No fillers.

Many years later, Mark Parker, president and CEO of Nike, asked Steve if he had any advice for him. Steve volunteered:

Nike makes some of the best products in the world—products that you lust after, absolutely beautiful, stunning products. But you also make a lot of crap. Just get rid of the crappy stuff and focus on the good stuff.

That's exactly what Steve was doing himself, except that the brutal truth was that much of Apple's entire product line had become "the crappy stuff." Quadrant by quadrant, he would soon fill his chart with groundbreaking new computers.

Steve's product plan was the foundation for a new Apple business model that would come to shake the world. By focusing on making fewer, higher-profile products, and by refusing to compromise on quality, Apple was able to achieve greater efficiency while it charged a premium price. Considering Apple had been losing money for some time, few observers would have predicted just how big an impact Steve's new approach was going to have.

As Steve often said, Apple is very good at saying no. It actively resists the temptation to make new products simply because it can. Judging by other technology companies' product lines, being that disciplined is a very difficult thing to do.

While Steve was busy minimizing, the rest of the industry was heading in the opposite direction.

The Perils of Proliferation

Imagine that you're eager to buy a laptop today. Your old machine just died, your pocket is stuffed with cash, you have a super-itchy "buy" finger, and you're ready to pounce on the first good deal you find.

Visit Apple's site and you can choose between two models: MacBook Air and MacBook Pro. Within each of those models, you can choose the size screen you want and make your choices for speed, memory, and disk size. Pretty simple.

Now take a look at the sites for HP and Dell. Their lineups change frequently, but in November of 2012, HP was offering forty-nine distinct models of laptops while Dell was offering forty-two. These computers have a range of overlapping features, and many are spread across different pages. I've yet to meet a human being who can explain why so many different models are necessary.

This is called product proliferation. Many companies can't stop themselves from responding to every opportunity, trying to please every customer and close every sale—when in fact they would be better served by making their product lineup logical and easier to navigate. They seem to forget that trying to please everyone is a good way to please no one. Choosing the path of Simplicity, Apple elects to do just a few things but do them incredibly well. It builds a large and loyal following not because of the products it *can* make but because of the products it *chooses* to make. It makes premium products only. It's happy to cede the market for low-end products to anyone who cares to take it.

Few shoppers at Dell.com understand why one model would be perfect for dad at the office but not so perfect for dad at home. Forgetting the whole "ease of use" thing, which often sparks debate between the Mac and PC crowds, which manufacturer makes the best case for "ease of purchase"?

Complexity loves nothing more than a sea of choices. It's enough to stretch your decision time from a few minutes to a few hours. It's enough to send you scurrying to the phone to call your expert friend or Googling buying guides in search of some confidence and peace of mind.

HP and Dell will explain that they make all these different models because their customers demand "choice." Apple's method is to offer distinct models with obvious differences (ultrathin and ultralight versus full-featured) and then allow customers to customize their choice to taste.

Customers hardly leave the Apple site feeling deprived of choices. Instead, they feel like Apple's product line was presented in a way that made their purchase simple. The experience of shopping for a Mac reinforces the image of Apple as the company that makes advanced computers easy to buy and easy to own.

Those who believe that a sea of models makes for happier customers would do well to look at the hard evidence. For nine consecutive years (up to 2012), Apple has finished ahead of all PC makers in the American Customer Satisfaction Index. A "lack of choice" has never been a significant issue. If anything, Apple's easy-to-understand product line has contributed to the company's consistently high ratings. Rather than seeing less choice, Apple customers see less confusion. They become attached to a company that gives them a simple shopping experience.

Certainly customers demand and appreciate choice—it's the overdose that becomes damaging. When choice becomes overwhelming, it ceases to be a benefit and starts to become a liability. It's a needless distraction for those who came to visit a site determined to spend their money. At a certain point, an overabundance of choice only torpedoes a person's ability to make a confident decision. For many, it even causes postpurchase angst, as they wonder whether they really bought the right thing.

Astoundingly, even some of Dell's own people can't explain the differences between models anymore. To better understand how Dell helps customers make decisions, I've done some "mystery shopping" with its sales reps, both online and on the phone. I start with a fairly basic problem: "I want a thin and light laptop, but I'm confused by the many different models on your site. Can you help me understand the differences?"

To Dell's credit, the reps have been consistently pleasant. To Dell's detriment, I've yet to hear any of the reps clarify much of anything. Their approach seems to be similar to the one Dell takes on its website: They throw a bunch of models out there and hope you like one. When, after explaining my priorities, I've tried to move things along by saying, "So which one do you think would be best for me?" I have received recommendations—but I've received different recommendations from different reps. Though I've posed as a customer who can't quite tell one model from the next, I'm not acting. It's confusing as hell.

The basic rule of business on the Internet is no different from the one in real-world stores. The faster and simpler you can make the buying experience, the more business you'll do. A goal for every online retailer is to minimize the obstacles that stand between their customers and the "buy" button. When Simplicity is part of the deal, it's just easier for the customer to arrive at a decision and whip out their credit card.

Regular customers of HP and Dell are well acquainted with their PC maker's website, so their experience may not be a negative. However, it might not be much of a positive either. Positive impressions are what drive people to share their experience with friends, family, and colleagues. Thriving in a competitive world isn't about achieving a joyous neutrality. It's about standing out from the pack and offering customers an experience they can't find elsewhere.

This is the lure of Simplicity.

Shopping at the online Apple Store or in a physical Apple Store is far from a neutral experience. People buy Apple products because they're innovative and simple, but they're propelled toward a purchase because the shopping *experience* is innovative and simple. Apple has minimized the choices, so it's easy to find the product that's best for you, even if you weren't sure of that before you arrived. Customizing is simple. Buying is simple.

For Apple, reinforcing its brand is simple.

The Less the Merrier

Apple's idea of Simplicity has evolved over the years, as has most everything on this Earth.

When you look at the sleek, spare, brushed-metallic lines of an iMac today, it's hard to imagine working on the original, plasticky iMac that was a landmark of Simplicity in its day.

The way Jony Ive designed technology, and the way Steve Jobs partnered with him, every detail was important and worthy of agonizing over for as long as it took. When Steve sat the agency team down to show us the first prototype of the second-generation iMac, he did so with the spirit of a proud father.

He directed our attention to the lower corners of the iMac enclosure, where the front met the sides. He explained how, in the original iMac, three separate pieces of molded plastic came together at this juncture, with a thin line visible between those pieces. In the new version, these corners were a single piece with no joints at all. No customer on earth would have noticed that improvement. But he told the story as if he were describing how Michelangelo had painted one section of the Sistine Chapel.

He loved the fact that they'd been able to minimize so ingeniously.

Today every Apple product serves as an example of Simplicity as well as a blueprint—though many don't seem to be able to read it. When iPad was unveiled, for example, critics complained that it was lacking in features. When competitors' tablets began to arrive, they'd added everything iPad was "missing" to make their devices more attractive to buyers: more ports, memory card slots, etc. Their additions didn't sell. It was the subtractions made by Apple during the design stage that customers found more appealing.

If you ever felt the urge to buy an iPod because it was so beautifully crafted, or if you felt compelled to own an iPad because of the way it responded to your touch, or if your friend's new iPhone suddenly made your own phone seem less interesting, you already appreciate the power of Simplicity.

At those moments, you might not have imagined that your feelings were relevant to your business. But the truth is, they're relevant to every business on earth.

It should now be considered a basic law of commerce: Simplicity attracts.

Simplifying the Target

Complexity is tremendously proud of its accomplishment in the PC world. Among Dell, HP, Acer, Samsung, and others, PC product lines are a masterpiece of confusion spanning several continents.

The PC companies are churning out different models of computers for small business, big business, education, government, and consumers of every stripe. They offer more choices now than ever before—and make very little profit on each.

Apple, anchored by its belief in Simplicity, has evolved in a very different way. Rather than splinter its computer-marketing efforts among different types of customers, it generally focuses on one. It simply sees its customers as people. It markets its products based on the belief that its customers aren't looking for a great home computer or a great business computer—they're looking for a great computer, period.

It's a vastly simpler way to sell a product—and more cost-efficient as well. Apple's one marketing message serves all, giving customers credit for having the intelligence to self-select the model that best meets their needs. Some home users may feel they need the higher-powered "Pro" machine; some business users may prefer the basic entry model. All is good.

Given that profit margins have become so small for companies like Dell, it's perplexing why they would continue to support such a large number of computer models for both business and consumer. What it boils down to is that they just can't stop themselves. Unlike Apple, which operates under a single P&L, Dell is split into divisions that operate independently of one another. The two biggest divisions are Consumer and Commercial. Each has its own management, its own goals, its own expertise, and its own line of computers. Executives care little about what happens to any division other than their own.

The Commercial side is where Dell makes most of its money. Business users buy PCs and servers by the thousands. So Dell cheerfully designs its business-oriented computers according to the demands of the IT managers who control millions of dollars in corporate IT budgets. On the Consumer side, it tries to be more whimsical and style oriented with such features as interchangeable laptop covers (something that would only make an IT manager's life more frustrating, trying to please so many different people).

But the computer market today is very different from the market that took shape decades ago. Businesspeople want the cool computer for work as much as they want the cool computer for home. And consumers are demanding the highest-powered computers so they can enjoy the newest entertainment options, edit their home movies, etc.

Apple sees this coming together of needs as license to market a smaller number of high-quality computers. But Dell continues to splinter its resources among different divisions, each supporting its own sprawling family of products. It's ironic that in a time when PC companies suffer from microscopic profit margins, they continue to organize themselves and sell computers in such an inefficient way. In Dell's case, there are laptops with very similar specifications offered by both the Consumer and Commercial divisions. They compete with themselves.

Working with Dell, I found that many of its managers understand and appreciate the rewards that come from Apple's simpler approach to product families and marketing. They openly express admiration for what Apple has achieved and offer up some ideas to help move Dell in a simpler direction. But Dell, like so many other companies (inside and outside of technology), has developed an immunity to Simplicity. Its internal structure has taken on a life of its own over many years, and only a mammoth companywide effort could produce meaningful change.

Remember, being complicated is easy. It's Simplicity that requires serious work. Minimizing product lines and consolidating target audiences requires an organization that's willing to take a long, hard look at itself.

And it never happens by itself. Simplicity needs a champion.

The Imaginary Heroics of Michael Dell

Long ago, when I was a beginner just learning the secret tricks of an advertising copywriter, I developed a strange affliction.

It happened only when I was working on a piece of business that was facing some horrible problem that seemed to threaten its very existence. For no apparent reason, I would start imagining the most spectacular way—and therefore the least likely way—that my client company might pull out of its tailspin and conquer the world.

Needless to say, my time serving with Dell's agency led to several such moments. Pondering Dell's severe case of product proliferation, the changing mood of computer buyers, how the stars might align in some magical way if Dell could only simplify and minimize, realizing that only Michael Dell had the power to change things, and further realizing that Michael had 1,001 better things to do than waste his time with his lowly global ad agency—it hit me.

The most wildly implausible thing that could *ever* happen to Dell would be for Michael Dell to become the revolutionary he used to be, to fly in the face of all expectations about how a PC company should act. I imagined that Michael Dell would become the "minimizing king." My fantasy went like this:

One day Michael would invite the world's press to an important event—much as Apple does—and journalists would eagerly journey from far and wide to hear his words. Oh, okay, so maybe he'd have to offer some door prizes to boost attendance at this point. But this is a fantasy, so just play along with me.

There would be live television coverage of the event. Much as the president of the United States can stand before the American people, rattle off the serious challenges that face the country, and offer up a bold plan to restore its greatness, Michael Dell would present himself in a similarly heroic fashion. With two flags behind him—the American flag and some Dell flag designed especially for the occasion—Michael would lay out his bold vision, backed up by wonderfully convincing facts.

He'd tell the inspirational story of how, when he was still in college, he started Dell with nothing but an idea—growing the company to become one of the most popular brands on earth. He'd describe it as a company powered by sheer smarts, one that had fulfilled its goal of putting advanced technology into the hands of ordinary people, empowering them to do wonderful things and, yes, even change the world.

He'd describe how, in the quest to be the world's best computer company, Dell had expanded its product line fifty times over since its founding, serving every kind of customer on the planet, from filmmakers, teachers, and restaurateurs to giant corporations purchasing tens of thousands of PCs.

He'd describe how businesses and individuals had all become so much more sophisticated, and how technology had branched out in so many exciting new directions, including smartphones and tablets.

He'd say that no company was better positioned to help all kinds of people bring the amazing power of technology into their lives than Dell. Then he'd pause. Right on cue, that nationalistic music in the background would pause as well. In this sudden silence, with an audience in rapt attention, Michael would look directly into the camera to make the announcement to end all announcements. He'd say that Dell was about to make truly radical changes to ensure that it could lead the world from this golden age of technology to an infinitely more empowering platinum age. Maybe even titanium.

Starting today, he'd say, Dell was radically cutting its desktops and laptops from fifty models down to six. By focusing the entire company's efforts on a smaller number of models, Dell would be able to provide the fastest, highest-quality computers and most amazing new mobile devices at truly affordable prices. He'd explain how the new streamlined product line would enable Dell to meet the needs of all its customers and guarantee the absolute best user experience for everyone.

He'd pause to show a few examples of some supersexy, thin, and light laptops and tablets that he was also announcing this day, and the audience would rise to its feet. The video behind Michael would be awesome. We'd see images of corporate users, moms and dads, kids and small businesses all over the world being empowered like never before. Dell and its customers, joined at the hip, discovering new worlds.

Michael would boldly proclaim that this was a brand-new Dell for a brand-new time, dedicated to surprising its customers with new thinking that better connected friends, families, businesses, and every kind of organization.

He'd say that the new Dell would be more customer-focused than ever—offering simple choices, easy-to-use computers, and ultraresponsive support.

(In his head, Michael would be savoring his spreadsheet-to-be, because he'd know that doing all of these things was going to cut his operating expenses by at least a third as it boosted sales.)

Michael's presentation would make headlines in every country. The press would debate the wisdom of Dell's surprising transformation. As happened to Steve Jobs when he returned to Apple in 1997, some would attack Michael for failing to realize that he was the problem in the first place and that the company would be best served if he'd just stay the hell out. Others would praise Michael, saying that he was the only person who could restore the magic that had been part of Dell when it was younger, feistier, and rolling in cash. Most important, Dell would be a news story. It wouldn't be aiming to be "relevant"; it would be aiming to make history.

In an instant, Dell would be seen as the revolutionary force in technology, defying the decades-long trend that has dragged PCs into a dark hole from which there seems to be no escape.

Oh, and then there would be the ticker-tape parade down New York's Canyon of Heroes, followed by Congress canceling the next election to appoint Michael Dell president by unanimous acclamation.

• • •

Now, back to reality. The point of this fantasy isn't that Michael Dell should really do these things. It's that minimizing can be a tremendously powerful tool—but often requires great audacity. One must have the determination to take action even if that action may upset a number of people.

Unfortunately, the desire to minimize does not necessarily come hand-in-hand with intelligence. Some of the most brilliant people on this planet can't stop themselves from overcomplicating the way they do business. Many believe that filling a large grid with products is the best way to win their customers' hearts. The reality is that providing too many choices is a quick way to drive people to confusion.

Minimizing is about being both smart and clear. It sometimes takes strength to make the necessary changes, but in the end it creates more effective companies—and more effective leaders.

Death by a Thousand Cuts

I get the feeling you don't have Michael Dell's issues. You probably don't need to worry about building tens of millions of computers. More likely your company is concerned with building ideas, and you'd profit handsomely from a few really good ones. You don't need to minimize a product line—you need to minimize your processes.

So let's thank Dell for demonstrating how to clutter up a product portfolio and bring back Intel to show us how to clutter up a good idea.

I don't mean to be facetious, but we do owe these companies a debt of gratitude. Because they operate on such a large scale, they make it easier to see what can happen when Complexity gains a foothold. And the more aware you become of Complexity's devious ways, the better equipped you will be to counteract them.

My Intel experience came as a shock, as I arrived at Intel's agency fresh from the vastly simpler world of Apple. During my time with Apple, the approval of an idea meant that the agency was cleared to start production. Steve Jobs trusted the agency to do its job. The next time he'd see us was usually when we returned to the Apple boardroom to share the finished ads. Steve had minimized the processes involved in creative development.

No such minimization was evident in the world of Intel, as the approval of an idea was really just the first step on a long and winding road. That company's system indicated a lack of trust, involving a series of checks and balances intended to ensure success. In fact, Intel didn't even trust itself to make a decision—it set up an elaborate global system of focus groups to make doubly, triply sure it would create the best possible ad.

Some of this resulted from Intel's global perspective. It was legitimately concerned that its ads be effective across multiple cultures. Apple had similar concerns, but it chose a simpler route. Rather than consuming itself with international focus groups and lengthy analyses, it would simply gather opinions from Apple people on the ground in different countries. If any issues were noted, we could deal with them.

Intel's reliance on focus-group testing was similar to that of other large companies. Its results were similar as well—for the most part, it ended up with ads that weren't terribly distinguished. This is often what happens when work is homogenized in an attempt to create "the perfect ad"—the one that hits on every important selling point and offends no one. Ads like this may produce the desired feedback in focus groups, but they often fail to make an emotional connection with the customer.

At Apple, selecting the best ads was a logical process, even if it did involve some passionate debate. Intelligent adults would sit around the boardroom table and discuss the ads' merits. (Except for the one time when Steve's then-nine-year-old son, Reed, was invited to weigh in on a new iMac campaign. He liked it.)

When I say that Intel was fond of focus groups, I'm actually understating its reliance on this tool. When we embarked upon a new campaign in Intel's world, here is how the development process normally worked:

- Pick the top three campaigns.
- Organize focus groups in several cities to test all three (internationally, when required).
- Produce the favored campaign (and sometimes the second-favorite as well, as a backup).
- Retest the finished versions of all ads with more focus groups.
- Revise the ads as necessary, based on the research.
- Run the ads on TV.
- Re-retest the currently airing ads, making running changes if needed.

Testing was a religion to Intel, just as Simplicity is to Apple. The reliance on focus groups was baked into the system, from start to finish.

Research like this was a mandatory part of every marketing project—and it clogged up the works mightily.

Intel had built a complete global research group into its organization, continuously testing campaigns all around the world. At critical points in the process, we would be summoned to a meeting, along with Intel's marketing executives, to get the full report.

The research people beamed with pride over some of their tests. In one, they would reduce a thirty-second commercial to thirty frames, one for each second. After the test subjects viewed the spot, they'd take them through each frame to see which ones they remembered. The result was a graph that showed, second by second, how memorable the ad was. This allowed them to point out exactly where the ad needed to be "beefed up."

This type of test seems to imply that the ultimate ad is one that hits a high note throughout its entire thirty seconds, which of course is not how good storytelling works. But this type of analysis was part of Intel's engineering DNA, and these meetings were built into the process. Going unnoticed was the fact that microanalysis of this nature was eating up time and money as it pushed the work toward mediocrity.

It also never dawned on Intel that just up the road a piece, at Apple's headquarters, these processes were absent, yet Apple was continuously turning out award-winning, highly effective work.

Intel's approach seemed based on the premise that a single bad idea would bring down the empire. Apple's approach embraced the idea that it's okay to make a mistake, that it's better to shoot for the stars and fall short on occasion than to burden itself with processes that drain the creativity from its ads.

The difference between the two companies' processes was the ability to minimize. Apple had it; Intel did not.

Steve Jobs looked at pretty much everything with the idea of cutting it down to its essence, whether it was a new product or a new ad. He had an instant allergic reaction to any suggestion that might add a layer of complication—like a focus group.

Chiat was fortunate to have Steve Jobs as a client, a man whose love of

Simplicity wouldn't allow outsiders to inflict their judgment on his ads. For those who are forced to go through the focus-group process, having a partner on the client side who shares your values is the best way to prevent great ideas from being derailed.

The agency Goodby, Silverstein & Partners in San Francisco had a famous "focus group moment" when it took over the advertising for Saturn. It created a groundbreaking ad called *Sheet Metal*. The entire ad featured human beings navigating the roadways in place of cars. Only at the very end did a real car appear, when the announcer said: "When we design our cars, we don't see sheet metal. We see the people who may one day drive them." It was a captivating anthem-like spot—and it bombed in focus groups. Most car companies would probably have killed it as a result. Fortunately, the agency never lost faith, and it had a client who was willing to overrule the research. The ad went on to achieve extraordinary success.

Those who believe in Simplicity believe that good ideas need to be protected from those who would do them damage. The best way to do this is to minimize the processes through which these ideas must travel.

Don't Bury Your Fact in Facts

Human beings are a funny lot. Give them one idea and they nod their heads. Give them five and they simply scratch their heads. Or even worse, they forget you mentioned all those ideas in the first place.

Minimizing is the key to making a point stick. Though this is Common Sense, it may also be the most violated principle in marketing or any other business. Your point will be more quickly understood, and more easily remembered, if you don't clutter it up with other points.

Strangely, some of the most brilliant people on earth sometimes need to be reminded of it. Even a certain someone who started that upstart technology outfit operating out of Cupertino.

At one agency meeting with Steve Jobs, we were reviewing the content of a proposed iMac commercial when a debate arose about how much we should say in the commercial. The creative team was arguing that it would work best if the entire spot was devoted to describing the one key feature of this particular iMac. Steve, however, had it in his head that there were four or five really important things to say. It seemed to him that all of those copy points would fit comfortably in a thirty-second spot.

After debating the issue for a few minutes, it didn't look like Steve was going to budge. That's when a little voice started to make itself heard inside the head of Lee Clow, leader of the Chiat team. He decided this would be a good time to give Steve a live demonstration.

Lee tore five sheets of paper off of his notepad (yes, notepad—Lee was laptop-resistant at the time) and crumpled them into five balls. Once the crumpling was complete, he started his performance.

"Here, Steve, catch," said Lee, as he tossed a single ball of paper across the table. Steve caught it, no problem, and tossed it back.

"That's a good ad," said Lee.

"Now catch this," he said, as he threw all five paper balls in Steve's direction. Steve didn't catch a single one, and they bounced onto the table and floor.

"That's a bad ad," said Lee.

I hadn't seen that one before, so I rather enjoyed it. And it was pretty convincing proof: The more things you ask people to focus on, the fewer they'll remember. Lee's argument was that if we want to give people a good reason to check out an iMac, we should pick the most compelling feature and present it in the most compelling way.

Steve didn't exactly break down and pledge never to question us again. However, he did appreciate the point. Lee's demonstration lightened the tone of the conversation and turned the tide for us. When we left the room, we had the go-ahead for a much simpler ad than the one Steve had in his head at the start.

I couldn't help but have flashes of that meeting when I found myself working at Intel's agency several years later. Sitting in an edit room looking at the final version of the first commercial in our new campaign, I got a horrible feeling in the pit of my stomach when I counted the things in the ad that we were asking our audience to absorb. The spot itself had four titles spread throughout, each one stating a product feature. Then, at the end of the spot, it had not one or two but *four* screens containing titles and graphics that wrapped it up.

At this moment, I wished Lee Clow could step in and throw his paper balls or, even better, Steve Jobs would show up and fire someone—except I realized that this particular someone might be me. Steve wouldn't have cared that we'd tried every argument to make the spot simpler. To him, that would only mean we'd failed.

But there was no Lee or Steve in this room. Instead, there was a team of expert marketers from the client and agency, most of whom were giving this ad an enthusiastic thumbs-up. And that was understandable. There was at least one element in there to please every stakeholder, each of whom needed to see a certain message or logo flashed on the screen.

Unfortunately, Simplicity can't just swoop in like Han Solo and save the day at the eleventh hour. Your message needs to be minimized from the start.

People will always respond better to a single idea expressed clearly. They tune out when Complexity begins to speak instead.

The Inexplicable Urge to Obfuscate

Minimizing is one good way to turn a complicated thing into a simple thing. It's not hard to understand why a company would pull out all the stops to accomplish this.

What's baffling is why a big company, presumably well staffed with smart marketing people, would go in the opposite direction, turning a simple idea into something perplexing.

I'm talking to you, Microsoft.

In 2007 I had the pleasure of being involved in the marketing of Mac OS X Leopard, which was released about ten months after Microsoft Vista.

This was terrific timing for Apple, because Vista was bombing and PC users were fleeing it in droves. It seemed like the perfect time to suggest to PC users that their best upgrade option might be to move to a Mac. So that I could more intelligently write the story, I had to immerse myself in the world of Vista.

My point of comparison was the Leopard upgrade, which was as simple as upgrades get. Apple offered only one version of Leopard, costing $129. That version ran on every Mac and made available every advanced feature.

Vista, on the other hand, was a madhouse. There were four versions covering a range of features and a range of prices, from $200 to $400. The least capable version was over 50 percent more expensive than Leopard, and the most advanced version was more than three times the price.

On the Leopard side, the upgrade process was thoroughly minimized to make things better for the customer. On the Vista side, the upgrade process was difficult—seemingly to make things better for Microsoft.

But that was then and this is now. Surely Microsoft learned from its Vista experience and simplified the process for later versions of Windows, right? Well, Windows 7 slimmed down from four versions to three, ranging in price from $200 to $300—far more than the $30 Apple was charging for its OS. Windows 8 isn't much better. Now it's down to Core and Pro versions, at $100 and $140 respectively. You still have to figure out which one you need. And the most advanced version of Windows 8 costs seven times more than the only version of OS X.

Minimizing the choices provides customers with a simpler path, a better value, and a happier frame of mind. It takes effort to cut out the layers of Complexity, sometimes tremendous effort—but as Apple knows, the payoff is a more honest and trusting relationship with customers. That relationship has lasting value. Conversely, charging excessive prices and offering confusing choices make customers feel like they're being squeezed for every extra dollar. Not a good recipe for long-term customer relationships.

Of course, the time for Microsoft to do something would have been back at the very beginning, when its plan was just a few scribblings on a whiteboard. One can only imagine the effort it would take to set things straight now.

The moral of the story: When in doubt, minimize.

Chapter 4
Think Motion

When Steve Jobs returned to Apple in 1997, the company was in critical condition. As Steve would say in a later interview, his assessment was that "Apple was about ninety days from going bankrupt."

Clearly, in Steve's mind, what had transpired at Apple in the eleven years of his absence wasn't all that smart. Thankfully, all of that was behind him now—except for one little bit of Gil Amelio's questionable judgment that was still alive and kicking.

As many companies do when faced with tough times, Gil had authorized his marketing people to go looking for a new ad agency. As if it were his agency's fault that Apple had gotten itself into the trouble it was in.

So as Steve was settling into his new responsibilities, it came to his attention that Apple was in the midst of an "ad agency review." At this point in time, more than twenty agencies had submitted proposals and the list had been whittled to twelve. From there, the plan was to have a "meet and greet" with each, narrow the list to five, then let them have a big shoot-out for the prize. It would have taken forever.

Steve would never tolerate such a big-company process. And Apple didn't have that kind of time to waste. So he hit this process with the Simple Stick, killing it instantly. The only thing Steve agreed with was the need to bounce Apple's current agency, BBDO Los Angeles. After all, BBDO was the agency brought in by Sculley—after he fired Steve's agency, Chiat.

Steve wanted to keep this process very simple. He wanted to work with a small team of smart marketers he could trust. And in keeping with the spirit of Simplicity, he wanted to put the plan in motion. Right now.

Simplicity Never Stands Still

Steve put in a call to his old friend Lee Clow at Chiat and invited him for a meeting. Lee then invited me to join, as we knew each other well and I had put in eight years working with Steve on NeXT.

That first meeting had an air of history about it, because Steve and Lee had become one of the more famous duos in advertising when they launched the original Macintosh—and here they were, ready to talk about joining forces again. They shared a man hug and the meeting began. Basically, Steve recapped Apple's situation and talked about fixing Apple one step at a time. The biggest problem, of course, was the product line. What he told us was consistent with what he had said in a *BusinessWeek* interview right before he'd agreed to return to Apple:

The products suck! There's no sex in them anymore!

Steve didn't just hand his business to Chiat. He was going to make us work for it. He had received an interesting pitch via FedEx from Arnold, a creative agency in Boston, and he wasn't counting those guys out. He wanted his marketing people to feel good about the choice too, so he asked us to think about Apple's challenge and come back with some ideas soon.

The relationship shifted into high gear that day and hasn't stopped moving since.

There was a lot of excitement within Chiat about the idea of getting Apple back as a client. The agency had been fired years before when Steve left Apple, and many in the ad industry had seen that as a great injustice, given the spectacular work Chiat had done over a period of years. This was a chance to set things right.

Lee put together a talented team that included Rob Siltanen, who at the time was the lead creative for the agency's Nissan work. I had a ton of respect for Rob, as we had previously worked together on Apple at BBDO during the Sculley days.

The Chiat team created some videos to explore possible directions for an Apple brand ad. Since Apple's very survival was an issue, one video imagined what the world would be like if the company were to disappear. It showed people taking down Apple signage, closing up shops, etc., after Apple had met its imaginary end. Its point was that without Apple, the world would lose a powerful ally of creativity. It was true, but not uplifting. Another was an early version of the *Think different* commercial about the "crazy ones" who change the world, set to the Seal song "Crazy."

Chiat's thinking was enough for Steve and his marketing group to feel the love. The agency was soon signed up as Apple's official marketing partner. The work we had already shared became the starting point for the *Think different* campaign that would play such a big role in the resurrection of Apple.

The really crazy part (crazy in a good way) is that absolutely none of this would have happened had Steve not blown up the snaillike agency search in progress. He put the process on fast-forward and got the work he wanted on the air in the time that Amelio's crew might still have been having meet and greets with candidate agencies.

Simplicity is a big fan of context. Even if Steve had thought a traditional agency search was a valid way to do business (which he didn't), he would never have consented to it given the urgency of the situation. Common Sense said it was time to accelerate the decision process and rely on his best available tool: a small group of smart people.

The Smart Timeline

Project timelines come in several varieties. They can be leisurely, compressed, relaxed, or impossible.

Though it may defy logic, the easiest way to screw up a project is to give it too much time—enough time for people to rethink, revise, have second thoughts, invite others into the project, get more opinions, conduct tests, etc.

Leonard Bernstein captured this thought perfectly when he said:

To achieve great things, two things are needed; a plan, and not quite enough time.

No doubt every industry has its own "perfect" timeline that allows it to get the best results with maximum efficiency. In my experience with technology companies, I found the perfect project time to be about three months. That was the amount of time it would take us to get from original briefing to final, finished work going live. Within that schedule we would develop ideas, share them with clients, respond to comments or concerns, and then move into production. Any less time and we'd compromise on quality. Any more time and we'd invite overthinking. I found this to be true whether we were working with difficult clients who weren't the most brilliant creative judges or working directly with someone as marketing-savvy as Steve Jobs.

Bernstein's quote cites two essential elements to achieving greatness. Those apply well to Apple's world, along with two addendums.

1. **Aim realistically high.** When Apple created the first iPod, it didn't set out to create a portable player that could accommodate music, movies, podcasts, and photos. It created a music player. The rest would come later. In other words, don't overreach—it's important to achieve greatness, but your project has to end on time and deliver what you've promised. (Obviously, you shouldn't underreach either. You can't be so "realistic" that you produce something lackluster.)

2. **Never stop moving.** The project begins on day one and should consume people from the get-go. No time-outs allowed. Only when people are kept in constant motion do they stay focused with the right kind of intensity. Work isn't supposed to be easy; it's supposed to be gratifying—and keeping the team in motion is what gets you there.

Apple has grown to the point where it does a tremendous number of things at once, and in doing so has built one of the world's great juggling acts. Apple lives in constant motion, it never stops thrilling its audience, and it never lets things get old. As fantastic as its inventions may be, Apple only occasionally bites off more than it can chew.

A refined sense of scheduling improved over many years is what allows it to pull this off.

Concentrating on building the best possible 1.0 product gives Apple a number of advantages beyond scheduling. It normally allows the company to create a product that's not only revolutionary, but illuminates an even more exciting path ahead. Apple's first modern revolution was iPod, the 1.0 version of which was (in hindsight) extremely limited. But it clearly pointed the way toward different types of media and a new world of accessibility.

Another good example is iPhone. The 1.0 version of this product didn't even support apps, which quickly came to be the most revolutionary part of the platform. The original idea was that Apple would support only web apps developed in Safari.

Creating products this way gives Apple the ability to "recycle" its leadership. Apple creates the revolution, then—while its competitors work to catch up to the 1.0 version—it's already at work on the 2.0 version. Whatever features might have been cut from the original idea become part of the starting point for the next iteration. Year after year, as long as Apple continues to innovate, it has the opportunity to renew its leadership.

Apple gets an interesting marketing advantage from these cycles as well. Since it falls upon Apple's competitors to prove they've created a better device, they normally gravitate toward specification-heavy advertising.

They feel obligated to point out that they have more megapixels, more USB ports, more whatever. Meanwhile, Apple continues to market its products as it always has in an emotional, human manner, pointing out benefits rather than specs. Unless it currently has a breakthrough technology, Apple takes itself out of the spec-comparison game—and makes a more meaningful connection with its customers.

Of course, as Apple continues to dominate in a category such as music players or tablets, time is on its side. The longer people live with their iPad, for example, the more locked in they become with the iPad ecosystem of apps and accessories.

Simplicity is hard to leave behind.

Thinking Different vs. Thinking Crazy

The best way to prove the power of Simplicity is to go out in the field and conduct a little experiment using the scientific method:

1. Select two companies in the same industry, one devoted to Simplicity and the other burdened by Complexity.
2. Give them the same project.
3. Sit back and watch the fun.

As fate would have it, I found myself a participant in exactly such an experiment, though admittedly I didn't know it at the time. In two different agencies, at two different times, working with two different clients—Apple and Dell—I was part of two teams given identical assignments. We were asked to create a new brand campaign.

The brand, as you know, is a company's most valuable asset. When you have a strong brand, you're at the top of the list when customers decide to buy. Not only that, but your customers keep coming back for more and tend to spread the good word to friends and family. If you *don't* have a strong brand—well, you're just one of the many slugging it out for customers day by day. People may see value in your products for the moment, but they'll toss you overboard in a nanosecond if they find a better deal with someone else.

Most important, a strong brand is like cash in the bank. When people trust a brand and see real value in it, they're willing to pay more for it. If you have a strong brand, as Apple does today, you can charge a premium price and people will line up to pay it. Profit margins are high. If you have a mediocre brand, the only way to attract customers is by lowering prices. Profit margins are low.

This, of course, raises a question: If building a great brand is so critical, and big companies have the resources to invest, why is it that some are successful in building a loved and respected brand while others seem to struggle mightily and never gain ground?

Obviously there can be hundreds of factors. But there are certain fundamentals that have to be in place, organizationally and philosophically, if a company is to have any hope of success. You can walk the straight path of Simplicity or choose the dark, winding road of Complexity.

Here is a comparison between my two similarly conceived adventures in branding with Apple and Dell:

Apple set out to create a brand campaign in 1997.
Dell set out to create a brand campaign in 2008.

Apple wanted to start its campaign immediately.
Dell pondered a schedule that would take months.

Apple's brand team was led by its CEO.
Dell's brand team was led by a committee.

Apple trusted a small group of smart people.
Dell trusted a small group of incompatible people.

Apple knew exactly who it was.
Dell needed to figure out who it was.

Steve Jobs was an active participant.

Michael Dell would look in when the project was complete.

Apple's brand team required only the CEO's approval.

Dell's brand team required each division's approval.

Apple took a month to conceive and create a campaign.

Dell required a month just to talk about strategies.

Apple ended up with the *Think different* campaign.

Dell ended up with a stack of presentation boards stored neatly in a dark closet.

Dell should be given credit for taking a bold step. Its brand had been weakened over the years, and it was out of character for the company to embark on any plan that didn't offer an immediate return on investment. This was to be the first brand campaign in the history of Dell.

Unfortunately, Dell had invited Complexity into the organization many years earlier. The two biggest divisions, Consumer and Commercial, had become separate kingdoms. Each had its own P&L, its own sets of priorities, even its own Dell logo. (One of the goals of the brand effort was to create a logo that would be acceptable to both divisions.)

Dell formed a committee to manage the creation of its brand campaign. The word "committee" is not usually associated with successful creative endeavors, and this project did nothing to change that. The Consumer and Commercial divisions were both represented—but they were represented by two sworn enemies. (Their rivalry had previously become so intense, management had actually sent them to counseling.)

Whereas all participants in Apple's brand project were focused 100 percent on promoting the high-level brand, participants in the Dell initiative were at least as concerned with the special interests of their own divisions. Each side was loath to grant concessions to the other. In fact, just a few weeks into the mission, while we were still discussing strategic directions, one participant confided that he had no intention of accepting the committee's recommendation. His division was firing on all cylinders and he wouldn't change for anyone.

As you can imagine, such attitudes would never have survived in Apple's world. Steve laid out his vision, and all participants were aligned with it. Had Michael Dell been in the room on that first day to read his team the riot act—to say how embarrassing it was that they couldn't even agree on a logo and demand that everyone put their differences aside to build a unified Dell brand—it might have been a different story.

But that didn't happen. So it came as no surprise when, over a period of several months, Dell's brand team meetings became fewer, until there were none at all.

Apple got it right by empowering a small group of smart people and creating a schedule that didn't allow the process to stagnate. With the full participation of Steve Jobs, we made decisions quickly. We went from zero to campaign in less time than I'd ever seen it done before.

Simplicity is a fundamental requirement when you're trying to achieve lofty goals. As Dell discovered, a fractured, leaderless group without an urgent mandate is Simplicity-proof.

The Search for Microsoft's Values

Just about every company has a mission statement of some sort—an official set of words that describes who it is, what it does, and its reason for existing. Most agencies would consider having this document to be an essential first step toward creating an effective brand campaign.

Yet no one ever bothered to ask Steve for a mission statement before we created the *Think different* campaign. That's because he had already given us a briefing from the heart, and even though the company was in serious trouble, its brand essence was well known. If anyone had asked him to hand over such a document, Steve would probably have considered it big-company behavior anyway. We might even have been fortunate enough to see his "rotating turret" in action.

Working with Dell was a different story. This was a company that wasn't very good at describing itself. Had it been able to articulate its brand essence, we could have begun working on a brand campaign immediately. Instead, we had to spend the first few weeks of our brand project figuring out who Dell wanted to be—because who it was at the moment wasn't working too well.

Microsoft is another company that's done its share of floundering over the years. Like Dell, it started out setting the world on fire, then somehow lost its direction. It's still huge and highly profitable, but many of its customers would probably find it difficult to define the Microsoft brand today. While it was once the innovator and setter of standards, Microsoft has lagged behind as revolutions have swept both the smartphone and tablet categories. This sad state is reflected in its stock price, which has been stagnant for over a decade.

Microsoft's marketing has been spotty for at least as long. Once in a while it manages to strike a chord, then before you know it, it embarrasses itself with something like the "legendary" pairing of Bill Gates and Jerry Seinfeld in a series of TV commercials. Efforts like these fall flat and leave people scratching their heads.

Microsoft didn't sprout these marketing problems overnight. It's been battling them for years. A former marketing manager for Microsoft tells a story about a critical time in the company's past, when new layers of Complexity caused it to drift. For the sake of our tale, let's call him Brian.

When he joined the company, Brian truly loved his job. What he liked most about Microsoft was that "they did things." That is, the company understood that it was part of a fast-moving industry and didn't waste valuable time getting hung up on debate. Like Apple, Microsoft understood the value of staying in motion. It was brash too. The executive team knew it could execute faster and smarter than its competitors and considered this one of their great strategic advantages.

Brian loved this aspect of life at Microsoft because it was in such direct contrast to his experience with HP when he worked with its ad agency. He had observed that at HP, process had become more important than progress. "It was all about when the next meeting was going to take place and what kind of muffins might be served with the coffee. There seemed to be more concern about HP than what was going on in its customers' world," he said.

It was the Department of Justice investigation of Microsoft that sucked the life out of the company over a two-year period starting in 1999. Fearful that it might run afoul of government investigators, the company became listless in its marketing efforts, with no clear direction forward.

After Attorney General Janet Reno took Microsoft to court, Bob Herbold, then Microsoft's COO, called a meeting of the minds to calm people down and get everybody on the same page.

The attendee list was a who's who of Microsoft communications, including the company's chief counsel and its head of PR. At one point, an executive with responsibilities in community affairs stood up to speak her mind. She painted a picture of a great company unfairly tarnished by the press. Microsoft was doing many good things in this world, she said, and the government simply didn't appreciate this. The situation was frustrating to all of those who believed in the goodness of Microsoft and the value this company brought to the world.

Her speech built to a crescendo. "They think we're up to no good," she said. "They don't realize that Microsoft is about positive things. We need to help them understand what our values are."

She paused briefly, allowing that thought to resonate in the room. Then she looked straight at the communications team and said: "What are our values? Are they written somewhere? Does anyone have them?"

In other words, the way forward was for Microsoft to express its values to the world—but even as a Microsoft executive, she wasn't aware of what those values might be. There was no magic document hidden on anyone's computer either. The company's values had never been codified.

From that point, it took Microsoft eighteen months to study itself, crystallize its values and decide what it stood for.

It might have been because of the DOJ legal action, or it might have been because of Microsoft's inability to maintain its focus. Whatever the cause, Microsoft had devolved. It had changed from a company that moved at light speed to a corporate behemoth that had somehow lost the ability to turn words into action.

It was a frustrating time for Brian and his team. But things were looking up for Complexity, which saw its opening and went for it.

Suddenly lacking confidence in Microsoft's internal marketing team, Steve Ballmer looked outside the company to meet this marketing challenge. He turned to polling expert Mark Penn in Washington DC to develop a positioning that would counter the growing public image of Microsoft as a dangerous monopoly. Penn was given the authority to develop a softer image for Microsoft and directed the marketing team to move in a whole new direction: The Microsoft brand would be about "kids, puppies and small businesses."

Inaccurate as the image was, it did follow a certain logic. If Microsoft wished to be seen as a softer, friendlier company, Penn knew that kids and puppies were slam dunks. A new emphasis on small business would logically counter Microsoft's image as a dark, dominating force.

Brian's marketing team was stunned. As far as they could tell, they didn't have the stories to support the new positioning. Small business, yes. But kids and puppies, no. The closest thing they had to a youth story was Microsoft's K–12 education software marketing program, which represented only a tiny fraction of Microsoft's market. Brian was responsible for the messaging to all of Microsoft's customers, and the warm/fuzzy approach seemed terribly out of place. However, the marketing group had now been expanded by one—an outsider whose expertise was not in marketing—and things would never be simple again.

Brian's experience continued to spiral. He found himself having to represent ideas he didn't believe in, which, as we know, is a gross violation of the principles of Simplicity. Brian found himself presenting Microsoft's new kids-and-puppies brand to a meeting of DC lobbyists summoned to Microsoft's headquarters. It was an all-star cast of extremists on both sides of the political spectrum, including Ralph Reed from the Christian Coalition and Victor Fazio from the left. Under pressure, Microsoft was forced to become an "equal opportunity" kind of company, offending no one. Brian was dispatched to stand up and say, "Here are our new technologies, here's why they're good for America, and here's how we're communicating our ideas to everyone."

When he left that meeting, Brian felt lost. He actually called his dad to say, "I feel like I'm working for a tobacco company." He didn't feel good about himself or his situation.

It's always shocking to learn that a company as successful or influential as Microsoft or Dell can run into trouble trying to define itself. But that's the kind of confusion that results when big organizations get bigger—and people lose sight of what makes things simple.

Chapter 5
Think Iconic

The *Think different* campaign consisted of a series of images of people who changed the world by "thinking different." On an ongoing basis, the agency had many memorable conversations with Steve Jobs about the types of people we might feature: scientists, astronauts, singers, directors, musicians, athletes, most every type of person, living or deceased. Once we'd settled on a person, we'd then take a look at the different images available, searching for the one truly iconic shot—the one that would conjure up a mental image of the person's life or accomplishments.

For me, the process itself conjured up an image from just a few years prior, when I was working with Steve on NeXT's marketing. When he was explaining the potential impact of NeXT's revolutionary software, he'd often make references to iconic people or periods in history. He would mention the Industrial Revolution to make a point about the potential impact of NeXT technology in creating a new foundation for building software. He would mention Shakespeare, whose entire collected works were included on the NeXT Computer. He'd bring up Henry Ford as he described the amazing robotic factory he'd built to manufacture his new computers.

That mental connection between his new days at Apple and his former days at NeXT made me remember an experience at NeXT that I could only appreciate in retrospect.

It was the summer of 1993, at least a couple of years before Steve would start planning his way back to Apple. I'd arrived at NeXT's Redwood City offices early for a creative meeting and was fortunate enough to get some private Steve time in his office prior to our meeting.

In those days, NeXT was in a constant state of struggle—but at least it was *supposed* to be in a state of struggle. NeXT was a start-up trying to convince the corporate world that it needed a different kind of computer. Apple, on the other hand, had no good excuse for its sorry state. It had floated for a while after Steve had been driven away, but now the negative news stories were becoming much more frequent.

Echoing in my head as I sat with Steve was the latest bad Apple report, which I'd heard on my car radio just an hour earlier. Apple's shares had plummeted 23 percent after it had announced the largest quarterly loss in the company's history. In addition to the earnings hit, Apple was also announcing a restructuring plan that would result in 2,500 workers being laid off. It was a devastating day for the once high-flying Apple, pushing the company closer to the brink.

I was working on the assumption that because Steve had been thrown out of the company he'd built from scratch, a place where he had invested all of his emotions, he might hold a bit of a grudge. But I was wrong. Thoughtlessly, I made a snide remark about Apple's misfortune. Rather than giving Steve any kind of satisfaction, it took the wind out of his sails. He went silent and stared down at his desk. He was genuinely depressed.

"Yeah, it's really, really sad," was all he could say, almost in a whisper.

I realized that revenge against Apple was not on Steve's agenda. Instead, I saw a father sharing the pain of his child. It didn't matter that there had been a split in the family—they were still family. Steve hated to see Apple going downhill like that.

I'd think about that day at NeXT when we were having those early *Think different* conversations at Apple. It was interesting to think that I'd seen Steve watching, powerless, as Apple was hurting, pained that he could not help—and now he was back where he belonged. The company that had once decided it didn't need him anymore now saw him as its last, best hope.

Steve's fascination with history and his appreciation for iconic images would figure prominently in the work that lay ahead.

The Seed of Apple's Rebirth

Steve's return to Apple in 1997 made headlines, as any news about Steve would make headlines. After all, he'd become an icon too. And his return to Apple was one of the juicier Steve stories to appear in many years. It had a bit of everything: the rise and fall of a great American company, a deal worth tens of millions of dollars, some brewing alliances and conspiracies.

At this point, Steve had been absent from Apple for eleven years, and it had become extremely clear what he had taken with him: the company's heart. Without Steve to personally guide and inspire the company, it was simply running on fumes. Each new CEO had tried to reinvigorate Apple, but none came close. Apple was losing its identity as a creative force.

My first association with Apple was during the time of Steve's absence, when John Sculley was CEO. As mentioned earlier, once Sculley had pushed Steve out of the company, he had wasted no time in replacing Steve's agency with his own. Chiat was out and BBDO was in. BBDO quickly hired Chiat's Steve Hayden, who had been responsible for the amazing advertising that launched the original Macintosh, to lead its creative team. And Hayden, bless his heart, allowed me to fulfill my dream of becoming a writer for Apple. But this was Sculley's Apple, not Steve Jobs's.

After a meeting in Cupertino, one of Apple's senior marketing people had given me his assessment of what life was like inside Apple with the new CEO. "It's like Sculley moved into a house that was all set up, with nice furniture in every room," he explained. "Things were fine for a while, but then you'd notice that familiar things were no longer where you thought they'd be. Or the drapes would get changed to something that didn't match the room. Or you'd notice some moving guys carrying a sofa away and yell, 'Hey, wait, that's my favorite couch!' but they didn't listen. Pretty soon, the whole place started to feel different. It was still the same house, it just didn't feel like home anymore. And your friends didn't want to come over anymore because it wasn't as much fun as it used to be."

Well, now Steve was back. Some believed that he was literally the only human being on earth who could have saved Apple, that only he could inspire the company's employees to greater heights. However, others weren't quite so convinced. Based on his past performances at Apple and NeXT, there remained the very real possibility that even Steve couldn't pull Apple back from the brink.

The challenge facing Steve was almost unimaginable. He had returned to become the leader of a brand that had literally ignited the personal computer revolution but was now in danger of becoming irrelevant. Even many who had once followed Apple religiously had given up hope. Steve needed to make the company command attention again. He needed to reassure the world that Apple hadn't lost its ability to innovate. He needed to reanimate the spirit that had created the revolution of Macintosh.

One can only guess how Apple might have fared had it decided to bring in some other CEO to tackle its problems. Normally, when a company is so close to disaster, management circles the wagons and insists on making whatever cutbacks are necessary to stop the bleeding while they figure out how to restore profitability. That wasn't Steve's approach at all.

Steve was willing to invest—not just in rebuilding Apple's product portfolio, but in rebuilding its image. He was so passionate about saving Apple, it was easy for the agency to get swept up in his plans—even if we had to go more on faith than on reality. We had a front-row seat to the famous Steve Jobs reality distortion field.

As noted in the previous chapter, it was in our first meeting, when Lee Clow and Steve were just exploring the idea of uniting once again, that Steve laid the groundwork for what would become our first assignment. He was clear that this was a perilous time for Apple, and that the company had been dying of neglect. The previous tenants did not understand the essence of Apple, nor did they have the vision that could restore it to health.

Though Steve's mission was to save Apple, he thought of it in even grander terms. He believed that Apple occupied a very special place in the scheme of things, especially when compared to the IBMs and HPs of the world. In his mind, we weren't just fighting for Apple, we were fighting for the spirit of creativity and innovation. If Apple was to disappear, he believed that those sacred values would be left without a champion in the computer category.

The biggest problem at that time was that Apple's products were entirely unthrilling. In Steve's absence, Apple had been unwilling to give up the dream that it could one day be embraced by business users. So the non-Steve management had shied away from the idea of making any computer that might turn off the business leaders it was trying to woo.

Totally out of character with the way the company had started, Apple was languishing in mediocrity. Sales were down. There weren't even any products on the drawing board with the potential to shake things up. The current product lineup wasn't creating lust in any kind of customer, business or consumer.

In Steve's briefing to us, he promised that things would change. Drastically. He asked us to believe that Apple was going to return to greatness by making great products. That was a given. His design teams were already working on that. Our challenge as an agency was to project a positive image to the world and reintroduce the spirit of Apple.

There would be at least a six-month period before the first of Steve's new products rolled off the assembly line. During that time, he wanted to start a campaign that would lay the foundation for Apple's comeback and set the stage for the innovative products to come.

Target-wise Apple needed to reach three different groups of people. First were those who remembered the great Apple of old but whose opinions of the brand had faded along with Apple's success. Second was the new generation of users who were young enough that they'd only known one Apple—the anemic one.

Third, and every bit as important, were Apple employees. They were in serious need of some inspiration after years of bad press, a succession of ineffective CEOs, and a lack of innovative products. Even so, Steve was upbeat about what he'd found upon his return. Despite the tough years, a lot of talented people had stayed at Apple because they believed in it, and they were just waiting for the chance to help make it great again. Steve believed that a great brand campaign would serve to rejuvenate the spirit of Apple inside the company.

Knowing that cool new products were to come, we were to create a brand campaign that would serve as the foundation for Apple's new wave of innovation. We would tell the world what Apple stood for and let the products that followed become the physical manifestation of Apple's brand.

We didn't know anything about "thinking different" at this point. We just had to start thinking.

Think Different: Birth of an Iconic Campaign

As previously noted, Lee Clow and Steve Jobs represented one of the most famous client-agency pairings of all time. Together they had created some of the world's best-known and most respected advertising efforts. You could see that they had great mutual admiration simply by the way they interacted. And they had plenty of good reasons to admire one another.

Chiat's work in launching Macintosh in 1984 was as historic as the computer. Apple captured the world's attention with its groundbreaking technology while Chiat's advertising boosted its own image as a West Coast creative powerhouse.

The pieces were certainly in place for Steve to get the brand campaign he hoped for. Now he had a great agency that shared his passion, the guidance of Lee Clow, and an energetic cast of characters for whom this would be a labor of love.

While some agencies think of a brand campaign as an opportunity to invent a new personality for their client, our task with Apple was to simply shine a light on the spirit that was already there. The ads had to be authentic. If this work was to truly define Apple, we knew that the "big idea" couldn't be complicated. It had to be direct, to the point, and simple.

Steve Jobs had already given us all the briefing we needed. Apple had always been "different"—and what drove it had never changed. The same spirit and values that created Macintosh in 1984 would lead Apple to create amazing products in 1998 and beyond. Apple wasn't for everybody; it was for those who valued creative thinking.

As the Chiat team generated ideas, two words made everyone take notice: "Think different." While every writer in the room would have liked to take credit for the phrase, it was actually the work of art director Craig Tanimoto. In those two words, Craig had managed to describe the essence of Apple. Those words would not only strike a chord with Apple's customers, they would serve as a battle cry for its employees.

If you believe that great companies are founded on a set of values that remain constant, then the perfect theme line is one that you could attach to the company at any point in its history. I think that's what I loved most about the words "Think different." I could imagine them hanging in the garage where Jobs and Wozniak had created their first computer as easily as I could imagine them driving the company in the present.

But the words became even more powerful when combined with images of people whose thinking had truly changed the world, like Albert Einstein. They seemed to both describe his life and celebrate it. This combination of words and images gave Apple a compelling way to relaunch its brand.

You can tell a lot about someone by the people he or she admires, and that would be the philosophy of our campaign. By celebrating the lives of those who inspired Apple, Apple would be telling the world exactly what kind of company it is—without using any more words than "Think different." We wouldn't be churning out ads. Instead, we'd be crafting posters that paid tribute to Apple's heroes.

We would choose iconic figures who stepped outside the bounds of conventional thinking in many different pursuits, including science, business, sports, and the arts. We would feature people as diverse as Albert Einstein and Jim Henson, Alfred Hitchcock and the Dalai Lama, Bob Dylan and Martin Luther King Jr.

The *Think different* ads were a vivid reminder that a single iconic image can be the most powerful form of communication. As we developed the campaign, each ad consisted of one black-and-white portrait of an Apple "hero," bleeding off all sides of the page, with nothing more than the Apple logo and the words "Think different" placed tastefully in a corner. On television, the commercial that launched the campaign similarly used black-and-white film clips that captured the spirit of each individual. Over this series of images Richard Dreyfuss read a script that praised the "crazy ones" who dared to see things differently.

The *Think different* campaign couldn't have been simpler. No matter where those black-and-white images appeared—in magazines, on posters, and on billboards—they registered with viewers in a nanosecond.

Not too many pages ago I talked about how important it is for the ultimate decision maker to take an interest in the process. In the making of the *Think different* commercial, Steve Jobs raised the bar for CEO involvement.

We were still working on the final edit of the ad in Los Angeles the night before Steve was to unveil the campaign during a 9:00 A.M. meeting of his global marketing team at Apple. So, several hundred miles north, Steve was sitting at home reviewing each version we created until we finally finished the job—at 3:00 A.M. Given that in those days we practically had to deliver such things by Pony Express, this was barely enough time to get the final version to Steve for his presentation. We were also racing a deadline with ABC TV, which was going to show the ad during the network TV debut of *Toy Story* on *The Wonderful World of Disney* a few days later.

One reason we kept Steve up so late was that we were debating the choice of voice talent almost to the last minute. In the preceding days, we had recorded a number of voices in a Los Angeles studio, including Richard Dreyfuss, Peter Gallagher, Sally Kellerman, and (no kidding) Phyllis Diller. But the agency was actually pushing for a voice I'd recorded up in the Apple auditorium a few days earlier: Steve Jobs himself. More on this later—but after a lot of discussion, we chose Richard Dreyfuss. He not only became our voice for *The Crazy Ones* but performed as the voice talent for a few Mac ads that followed.

After that very late night, a noticeably tired Steve Jobs showed up for his meeting the next morning. Fortunately, a tired Steve Jobs was more riveting than most wide-awake CEOs. His introduction of the campaign to this group is thought by many to be a perfect presentation about the power of brands. Considering that marketing can be a murky, perplexing profession filled with opinions and theories, Steve made it sound simple. Here's what he said:

> To me, marketing is about values. This is a very complicated world, it's a very noisy world, and we're not going to get a chance to get people to remember much about us. No company is. And so we have to be really clear on what we want them to know about us.
>
> Now, Apple—fortunately—is one of the half a dozen best brands in the whole world. Right up there with Nike, Disney, Coke, Sony. It is one of the greats of the greats. Not just in this country, but all around the globe. But even a great brand needs investment and caring if it's going to retain its relevance and vitality, and the Apple brand has clearly suffered from neglect in this area in the last few years. And we need to bring it back. The way to do that is not to talk about speeds and feeds. It's not to talk about MIPS and megahertz. It's not to talk about why we're better than Windows. The dairy industry tried for twenty years to convince you that milk was good for you. It's a lie, but they tried anyway. [Audience laughs.] And the sales have gone like this [down], and then they tried "got milk?" and the sales have gone like this [up]. "got milk?" doesn't even talk about the product—matter of fact the focus is on the absence of the product.
>
> But the best example of all, and one of the greatest jobs of marketing that the universe has ever seen, is Nike. Remember, Nike sells a commodity. They sell shoes. And yet when you think of Nike, you feel something different than a shoe company. In their ads, as you know, they don't ever talk about the product. They don't ever tell you about their air soles and why

they're better than Reebok's air soles. What does Nike do in their advertising? They honor great athletes, and they honor great athletics. That's who they are, that's what they are about.

Apple spends a fortune on advertising. You'd never know it. . . . So, when I got here, Apple [had] just fired their agency and was in a competition with twenty-three agencies that, you know, four years from now they'd pick one. And we blew that up and we hired Chiat/Day, the ad agency that I was fortunate enough to work with years ago, who created some award-winning work, including the commercial voted the best ad ever made, 1984, by advertising professionals. . . .

And we started working with that agency again, and the question we asked was: Our customers want to know, "Who is Apple, and what is it that we stand for? Where do we fit in this world?" And what we're about isn't making boxes for people to get their jobs done, although we do that well. We do that better than almost anybody in some cases. But Apple is about something more than that. Apple at the core, its core value, is that we believe that people with passion can change the world for the better. That's what we believe. . . . And that those people who are crazy enough to think they can change the world are the ones that actually do.

And so what we're going to do in our first brand marketing campaign in several years is to get back to that core value. A lot of things have changed. The market is a totally different place from what it was a decade ago. And Apple is totally different, and Apple's place in it is totally different. . . . But values—and core values—those things shouldn't change. The things that Apple believed in at its core are the same things that Apple really stands for today.

And so we wanted to find a way to communicate this. And what we have is something that I am very moved by. It honors those people who have changed the world. Some of them are living; some of them are not. But the ones that aren't, as you'll see—you know that if they ever used a computer, it would have been a Mac. The theme of the campaign is Think different . . . *honoring the people who think different and who*

*move this world forward. And it is what we are about; it touches the soul
of this company. . . . I hope that you feel the same way about it I do.*

Seeing the Big Picture

A company facing extinction will normally do whatever it takes to keep
itself alive—anything except increasing marketing costs, of course.

After all, it's the lack of money that's about to make the company go
belly up. Since marketing schemes don't usually come with a guaranteed
return on investment, they require a leap of faith—and faith is a hard sell
to management during a crisis.

So it takes a large degree of nerve to pour a good chunk of what's left
into something as intangible as a new brand campaign. But that's just what
Steve did. In a certain way, he seemed to feel liberated by Apple's predica-
ment. He made it clear that Apple couldn't be withdrawing into a shell at
a time like this—now was its last chance to get out there and put its stake
in the ground. The company had to invest in itself.

And invest Steve did.

As he noted when he presented the *Think different* work to his marketing team, "Apple spends a fortune on advertising. You'd never know it." By
this he meant that Apple had a large budget for advertising, but it had squan-
dered it. It had let Complexity get in the way. Apple was trying to advertise
so many products with that budget, it was saying a hundred things quietly
instead of one thing loudly.

Over the course of the next year, I would marvel at how bold Simplicity could be. Rather than advertise a variety of products, Steve insisted that
there be a single focus for every quarter. That focus would be highlighted
on the apple.com home page and it would be the subject of almost all of the
advertising. The effect was impressive. By saying fewer things in more important places, Apple seemed to get more notice than companies like IBM,
which had a vastly larger marketing budget.

The *Think different* campaign was Steve's first big marketing expendi-
ture during his new reign at Apple. Chiat's media chief, Monica Karo,

earned his respect by creating a media plan that was as simple and compelling as the images in the campaign. It wasn't cheap, but Steve knew it was right. He recognized the power of these iconic images to stop people in their tracks.

Monica made sure that the *Think different* campaign appeared only in those places where it would achieve maximum notice, and never in places that would degrade the message. These portraits of *Think different* heroes never ran on the inside pages of a magazine. They ran only on back covers, where they would shine on their own. They were a common sight on coffee tables in homes and businesses. But it was out in the real world that the ads had such a commanding presence. Billboards became a huge part of the effort—but only in the most prime locations. Apple started systematically locking up the most visible billboard locations all over the United States as they became available—near airports, approaches to major cities, etc. In urban environments, Apple's images appeared on bus shelters, using back-lit posters that stood out in the night. Most strikingly, *Think different* images were painted onto the sides of large buildings. In New York City, the classic photo of John and Yoko in bed stared down upon passersby. Just John, Yoko, and those simple words, "Think different."

Steve approved all of this with great relish—and, of course, without testing any of the ads beforehand. In his heart he knew this work would resonate with the intended audience. With no time to spare as Apple tried to rebuild, he had no interest in looking before he leaped. He would certainly not let a focus group dictate the message Apple would broadcast to the world.

Simplicity's Unfair Advantage

There's a reason why, even in the best of times, most companies are leery of running a pure brand campaign. That's more a long-term thing than a short-term thing. Especially in tough economic times, most corporate leaders would choose the quicker profits in a heartbeat.

Selling a brand campaign to a client is often like selling a nineteen-year-old on the benefits of starting a retirement account. The gains are just too far off in the future. They're in business to make money now.

Sometimes, some very confident agency people tell their client that they have the smarts to take care of the long-term and short-term needs all at the same time—selling the products hard while they build a strong brand. It's a neat trick if you can do it, but few actually do.

By sticking to its beliefs, Apple has achieved what is truly the holy grail of advertising. It's built a line of products that are the personification of its brand. Every day Apple is out there selling its products hard, yet every sale reinforces the Apple brand—giving customers more reason to believe that Apple is the company that cares most about design, advanced technology, and Simplicity.

Back at the very beginning, when Steve Jobs gave the agency team his briefing, we knew that the brand campaign was to be the beginning of a transformation. We knew that the proof of *Think different* would be evident in revolutionary products to come, the first of which would be the new home computer.

At that time, we had no idea what iMac was going to look like. We were working on faith that it was going to be special. Sometimes the stars just align perfectly. We spent the first six months of our relationship with Apple branding the company with the words "Think different." And when the time came to launch the first new computer under Steve's watch, it couldn't have paid off that theme line any better.

As an icon of Apple's rebirth, iMac worked beautifully. It was a visually stunning departure from every computer that had come before. In a world of boxy beige computers, iMac was translucent Bondi blue, allowing its inner circuitry to become part of its design. Honestly, all we really had to do was run a photograph of iMac under the headline "Think different," and that would have told the whole story. In the annals of electronics history, I don't believe there's ever been as effective or appropriate a branding buildup to a product release than *Think different* was to iMac.

Like the *Think different* ads, iMac ads featured one simple visual. The image of that computer, strikingly different from all PCs, was all we needed to rivet a reader. The iMac itself became a *Think different* personality—again proving the power of an iconic image. We did add some descriptive words on the product ads, but even then they were minimal.

Of course, iMac was only the start.

A new series of product launches followed, each building on Apple's different way of thinking. About a year after iMac came iBook, which, laughable as it may look by today's standards, brought iMac magic to the laptop category. It was the first mainstream computer to feature built-in Wi-Fi. There was Steve, standing onstage, accessing the Internet—*without wires!* For many it was the equivalent of seeing a lightbulb for the first time. Then came the radical new Mac Pro tower configuration and beautifully designed black PowerBook.

"Think different" quickly morphed from words that explained the company philosophically to words that perfectly described each new product as it was unveiled. Every Apple product broke new ground in some important way, and every ad relied on the power of a single striking visual. The photography was all-important, and that gorgeous imagery was enhanced with Apple-clever headlines. These were product ads in the classic sense—but given the brand image Apple had chosen to create, they were simultaneously brand ads as well.

In fact, we stopped running the *Think different* hero ads as Apple's new products began to roll out in quantity. Apple did not have to splinter its marketing dollars to run a brand campaign in addition to a product campaign. It had only one campaign. And every Apple product sold contributed to the brand image.

Of all the ways Apple has leveraged the power of Simplicity, I believe this was the most stunning demonstration of all.

Apple branded itself using iconic images and two words that perfectly described the spirit of the company. Following that initial investment, it would never have to invest in a traditional brand ad again. Every product became a manifestation of the Apple brand.

One Button: The Official Symbol of Simplicity

Without question, one is the simplest number ever invented. It's so simple, a child can understand it. The further away you get from one, the more complicated things get.

That's why Steve Jobs insisted on iPhone having only one button, rejecting many different models before arriving at the final version. You don't even have to use an iPhone to get that it's simpler. That visual cue—the single button—says a ton all by itself. In fact, one could say that the single button has become an icon of Apple's devotion to Simplicity.

Remember, before iPhone came along, all phones—especially smartphones—had buttons out the wazoo. Ultimately, through repeated use, you'd learn which button did what and where it was located, but it required some effort.

Simplicity requires little effort.

With iPhone, Apple staged a direct frontal assault on multibutton thinking. Part of it was purely psychological. After all those years of using phones populated with so many buttons, iPhone screamed Simplicity. It felt good to hold it in your hand, with your thumb poised over that one button. At the same time, it was comforting to know that no matter how deep you got into your iPhone, you could always return to the safety of home by pressing that same button.

But there are three functions that people use most on their iPhones: Internet, phone, and iPod. Three is a pretty small number. When they were designing iPhone, why didn't they just put three beautiful buttons at the bottom of iPhone instead of one? Arguably, that would have provided even quicker access to each of the main functions, and it still would have been an improvement over previous smartphones.

There's only one reason I can offer: Three is more than one.

To go that route would have resulted in an iPhone that was almost perfect. But Steve Jobs never dealt in "almosts." This unwillingness to compromise reflected the purity of his devotion to Simplicity. And the result—a revolution in the smartphone category—speaks volumes about the correctness of his philosophy.

When it comes to design, Apple carefully calculates the messages that will be sent by every product, even those messages that are mostly subconscious. It considers every aspect of a product's design: how it looks, how it feels, how it makes *you* feel. Part of the idea is to win you over before you even touch it. One button does an excellent job of that.

The designing of iPhone was not the first time that Steve Jobs put his foot down about this kind of Simplicity. A former director of product marketing at Apple, Mike Evangelist, has told the story of one of his first meetings with Steve Jobs, a meeting that took place in 2000 inside the Apple boardroom.

Mike's team had been charged with developing a simple way to turn a home movie into a DVD, an app that would later show up as iDVD (one of the iLife apps). He and a partner worked hard to develop their ideas for an interface that would be user-friendly enough for Steve, and prepared to share their work with him by creating all kinds of sample screens and verbal explanations.

Mike was shocked when Steve Jobs walked into the room, ignored their work, and walked right up to the whiteboard.

"Here's the new application," he said. "It's got one window. You drag your video into the window. Then you click the button that says 'Burn.' That's it. That's what we're going to make."

As he tells the story, this left Mike dumbfounded. Never in all his experience had he seen software designed quite like this.

Clearly, if Apple had its way, all of its products would feature a single button. Now that Siri, the voice-controlled intelligent assistant, is here, you might want to prepare yourself for Apple products with zero buttons. After all, zero is the only number that's simpler than one.

Bringing Icons to Life

For many agencies, clients, and students of advertising, Apple is considered the gold standard in marketing. That's because Apple rigidly enforces the principles of Simplicity whenever it speaks to its customers.

Many of its product ads simply show a brief demonstration of the device. You might see Mr. Hand holding an iPhone, moving from one app to the next, or observe an iPad being demonstrated in much the same way.

The company has a formula of sorts, but simply showing the product isn't always it. What Apple has done with great success at key points in its history is create an image that becomes an icon for its product or product line. This image changes the way customers think about the technology, imbuing it with a personality that makes it harder to forget.

The ads for iPod are an interesting example of how Apple chose not to show its product at all but created iconic images that would be infinitely more effective. Unfortunately, en route to advertising greatness Apple did stumble out of the gate in its advertising for iPod.

The very first ad for iPod showed us a young guy in his apartment listening to music on his iMac. He plugs in his iPod, transfers a song from iMac to iPod, dons his iPod earphones, then keeps listening to the music as he boogies (literally) out of his apartment. It was somewhat uncomfortable to watch, and on the web some started referring to it as the "iClod" commercial. One problem with this ad was that it tried to layer some kind of artificial amusement on top of the product. That isn't necessarily an ad killer in itself, but in this case the amusement wasn't very amusing. It was a young guy trying to act cool and doing so in a fairly pitiful way.

Another problem was the "real person" aspect of this ad. In the past, Steve had often avoided the use of people in his ads because an actor who seemed cool to one viewer might be a turnoff to another. It's a challenge to find that one person with universal appeal (as the "iClod" proved).

This is a perfect time to pause and appreciate what we were talking about before—that Apple tests none of its ads, while big companies like Intel tend to test them all. Had Apple put this ad into testing, it might well have discovered that the ad didn't resonate in the way it had hoped. Maybe it would have killed the ad and done something else. Maybe. But when you stop to think of the hundreds of ads Apple has run over the years, and all the time and money (multiple millions) it would have cost to do all that testing, the correctness of Apple's approach becomes more apparent. Apple lets Chiat shoot for the stars. If it produces a clunker along the way, the world isn't going to end. People aren't going to abandon their Apple equipment on the streets. The ad might not have been great compared to previous efforts—but life goes on and Apple would simply try to do better next time. In the case of iPod, it would do fantastically better next time.

The campaign that ran for years after the first iPod ad transcended both problems contained in that ad. It had a hook that really was captivating, and it didn't try to impress us with the coolness of any particular person.

Instead, it did what Apple does best. It created an iconic image that came to immediately communicate "Apple" and "iPod." But at the same time, it broke some old Apple rules and looked like nothing that had been done before. Susan Alinsangan, a Chiat art director, came up with the design of the iPod *Silhouettes* commercials. This was a career highlight for Susan and she deserves all the praise she's received for it. Like the failed commercial that came before, the new campaign focused on people dancing—only this time the ads were stylized in such a way that you saw only two-dimensional silhouettes of people as they danced against brightly colored backgrounds. There was no product photography at all—only a white silhouette of iPod and its iconic white earphones.

This became the official look of iPod advertising, which appeared not only in TV ads but also on Apple's favorite medium, outdoor advertising. For years, billboards and bus shelters carried the iPod *Silhouettes* ads, which, due to their intense colors, were strikingly gorgeous when backlit at night, seemingly visible for miles. The iconic look of these ads became instantly recognizable to anyone exposed to the marketing effort—which was pretty much everyone on earth.

Considering the elegant design of iPod, it was a radical approach for Apple not to show the product at all. Especially when most of its other ads did nothing *but* show the product. Instead of asking you to buy this device, Apple was asking you to buy the emotion. Since iPod was all about music and joy, each ad simply conveyed the idea that someone was loving their iPod—without any need to show who that person was. These were incredibly human commercials, yet they never showed a human face.

Simplicity wins again.

To say "it worked," of course, would be an understatement. Certainly iPod is one of the most extraordinary successes in the history of Apple—and in the history of consumer electronics. Coupled with iTunes, a simple source of music (and ultimately movies, games, podcasts, radio broadcasts, and more), iPod still owned over 70 percent of the market more than ten years after it was introduced.

There was never really a serious challenger to iPod. Competitors came and went—including Microsoft's failed Zune—but none of them put a dent in iPod's mammoth market share. Only when the function of iPod began to be taken over by iPhone and iPad did sales begin to show signs of slowing. That has to be attributed to one of the strongest subbrands Apple has ever built—and one of the most iconic images it has ever created.

All that said, this campaign provides an insight into Steve Jobs and just how human he was. On occasion, he could actually be wrong.

Steve was a tough judge of advertising, as we know. One of his favorite comments after reviewing an ad was "You can do better." You might well end up where you started, with Steve agreeing with you enthusiastically, but you'd often get a good workout along the way. It was all part of the pursuit of greatness.

When the agency first shared the *Silhouettes* campaign with Steve, he didn't like it. It's not hard to understand why. It didn't look anything like any of the ads that Steve had approved in the past—which were mostly white pages featuring a product image and a clever headline. In that sense, it was "off brand." There was no stunning product shot. Not only was there less white space, there was absolutely no white space (unless you want to count the silhouette itself). "It's not Apple," said Steve.

In a case like this, the only thing you could do was stick to your guns, keep the debate going, and hope the campaign idea would work its way into Steve's comfort zone. The good news for Susan and her fellow creatives at Chiat was that Steve ultimately did come around.

Flash forward a year or two to one of the Macworld shows in San Francisco. I was on hand that day when Steve told the crowd that Apple had two new iPod ads. "Do you want to see them?" he asked, and the crowd went bonkers. I watched Steve's face as he stood there taking in the applause before and after he showed the commercials. He looked as happy and content as I'd ever seen him. He was truly proud of those spots.

Iconifying the Enemy

The nature of advertising is to claim that you have a better product. And when you're the underdog, as Apple has always been in the PC marketplace, one effective way to do that is to directly compare yourself to the leader.

How you portray your "enemy" has a big impact on how your audience perceives you. You can appear to be honest and good-natured or, if you're not careful, you can look condescending or mean.

In its history, Apple tried on several occasions to go up against Microsoft, without any significant results. A number of talented creative people gave it their best. In a series of spread ads in magazines and newspapers long ago, Apple compared "The hard way" on the left to "The easy way" on the right. You guessed it: Mac was the easy way. Logically, the ads made perfect sense. Emotionally, they just didn't connect. The reader saw two computers and a bunch of words. Given that Apple was such an underdog in those days, not a lot of people were convinced.

Years later, Apple would prove that it's all in the delivery. Thanks to Chiat's creative genius, the *Mac vs. PC* campaign would become what many consider the most hard-hitting and successful campaign in Apple history. It worked because it didn't try to be so literal in visualizing Microsoft as a screen on a computer. It turned both the Mac and PC platforms into human beings. Each was given a personality, and their interaction humorously drew attention to their differences.

Unlike the "hard way vs. easy way" approach, *Mac vs. PC* generated tons of interest. It became a frequent topic of conversation and the subject of countless YouTube parodies. The secret was in finding icons to represent the two sides of the argument instead of using real computers—and in this case, the icons were people.

Back in 1999, Apple found itself in a situation where it chose to battle an even bigger competitor: the entire world of computers. The story dominating the news that year was the dreaded Y2K bug, which threatened to cause a worldwide computer meltdown on New Year's Day 2000.

The problem was that most computers treated dates as two-digit numbers (representing "1999" as "99," for example), and were ill prepared to deal with the change from "99" to "00." Many computers would see "00" as "1900"—or even "19100"—and businesses feared chaos would result. It's impossible to pin down exactly how much money was spent to head off the problem, but it was massive. Global estimates range from $300 billion (International Data Corporation) to $600 billion (Gartner Group).

Steve Jobs was tickled by this, because those who relied on Macs didn't have to spend a cent. Macs were configured so that users wouldn't have any date-related issues until the year 29,940. After that, they'd be on their own.

Douglas Adams, author of *The Hitchhiker's Guide to the Galaxy* and an Apple fan, wrote a beautifully self-deprecating headline and sent it directly to Steve Jobs for Apple's use. It read:

We might not get everything right, but at least we knew
the century was going to end.

We used Adams's line on the web. For TV we searched for a way to best visualize the problem. Ultimately, we came up with a way to graphically depict the entire global mess using a simple red lens. Our spokesperson would be HAL, the menacing computer from *2001: A Space Odyssey*.

The beauty of HAL was that he lived in the year 2001, so unlike the rest of us, he'd already lived through the Y2K bug. He had suffered it himself.

HAL was a perfect image for a complicated problem, capturing the malevolence lurking in the PC world. The entire ad consisted of a slow move into a close-up of HAL's red eye.

It took some doing to get HAL on board, as the rights were jointly owned by MGM and Stanley Kubrick. MGM agreed quickly, but Kubrick was in London doing postproduction work on *Eyes Wide Shut*. We had to wait for him to surface, but when he did, he became a fan of the spot. (This despite the fact that the video we sent featured only a still image of HAL and me doing my best HAL impersonation.)

The only stick-in-the-mud was actor Douglas Rain, who played the voice of HAL in both *2001* and *2010*. He was an artist. And artists don't do ads, even if Kubrick says it's okay. So seventy-five auditions of HAL imitators later, we stumbled upon Tom Kane, who played C-3PO in Lucasfilm computer games and plays Yoda in the animated *Star Wars* TV series. He was well experienced in space and could do an impeccable HAL, right down to his slight Canadian accent.

The HAL ad ran during the Super Bowl in 1999, immediately following kickoff. Simplicity stood out once again—even if it was surrounded by beer commercials.

Chapter 6
Think Phrasal

The lump on the table was truly mysterious and held everyone's rapt attention. Hidden under a gray sheet it was impossible to discern any detail from it. We were going to have to wait for the big reveal when the meeting was called to order.

This would definitely not be our typical product briefing. Beneath that sheet was the home computer that was going to save Apple.

Not to get overly dramatic about it, but that's exactly how it was billed by Steve himself. This was the product that Steve had alluded to back when we had first started on the *Think different* campaign. He had told us that the first product out the door was going to be a rethinking of the home computer. He had given his engineers and designers the challenge to do something great, and now at long last we were going to see it.

There would be no saving Apple by churning out more beige boxes that failed to distinguish themselves, by looks or function, from the hundreds of PC models out there. Steve wanted this first product to open people's eyes and serve notice that Apple was back.

It was the spring of 1998, and we'd been summoned up to Cupertino for our first viewing of this new computer, code-named C1. The "C" stood for "consumer." Apple didn't use a lot of creative firepower on code names back then.

By this time we felt like we were already well along a journey, having developed the *Think different* campaign and placed it strategically on TV, billboards, and magazine back covers around the world. That was the brand-building part, and this was the real thing—a product that would prove that our brand campaign wasn't just a lot of advertising fluff.

Now we were sitting just a few feet from C1, anxious to see the results of all this reimagining. If Steve really was betting the company on this computer, it had to be brilliant. Apple was out of time, and this was the one shot it had to turn things around.

The agency delegation numbered five or six, consisting of creative people and account managers. There were two Apple product managers there to guide us. After some introductions and opening remarks, it was time to get down to business.

One product manager reached for the sheet and revealed C1.

There it was—the computer you'd come to know as iMac—looking like it came right out of *The Jetsons*. The group let out a collective "holy cow" and simply tried to absorb and appreciate what we were seeing—because it shattered every idea of what computers were supposed to look like. It was a colorful one-piece computer that showed off its inner circuitry through a semitransparent shell.

I'd like to believe we were all so smart that within seconds we were convinced that we were witnessing the start of a miracle resurgence. But it wasn't quite like that. Later, when the agency team was alone and able to share the thoughts we felt at that moment of reveal, we found that we all had pretty much the same feeling. It was part shock, part excitement, and part hope that Steve Jobs really knew what he was doing—because there was a real chance that this revolutionary computer might just be too shocking for its own good.

But the shape and design of C1 were only part of what was revealed that day. Along with C1 came an amazing new mouse. Just as the computer didn't look like anything we'd seen before, neither did the mouse. It was designed in the same friendly colors of the iMac, and it was round. "That's wild," we thought. It also turned out to be very dumb—but let's save that story for later. And sitting on a table along one wall of the room was still another computer under wraps. We were so wowed by the one before us, it never even dawned on us that there might be a sibling.

This turned out to be the pro tower model that would be announced soon after C1, the new Power Mac G3. It wasn't translucent, but it shared many of the C1 design features. It had lots of plasticky curves, including large handles on the front and back edges of the top.

The Power Mac G3 came with a large stand-alone display that was cut from the same cloth. Because it was also a CRT model requiring a ton of room in the back, this display was huge and bulbous, all decked out in blue and white plastic. More *Jetsons*. And decidedly less attractive. And it would ship with the same round mouse designed for C1.

We had similar "wows" upon the first reveal of the Power Mac G3, but this one made us a bit more nervous. Though it was aimed at pros, it looked very much like a consumer machine. The blue was gaudy. Clearly, design chief Jony Ive and his team had gotten superexcited about this new iMac design theme and were maxing out on it. Once again, that "Sure hope Steve knows what he's doing" thought popped into our heads.

It turns out, of course, that Steve really, *really* knew what he was doing. He didn't get it all exactly right, but he got so much of it right that he made computer history.

At our next meeting with Steve, he was eager to hear what we thought of C1. He was like a proud father. This was the main focus of Apple, and clearly Steve had poured his heart into its creation. He loved every detail and was eager to share it with the world. "The back of our computer looks better than the front of their computers," he said, a line he would repeat often. At this point, we'd had time to digest what we'd seen. Once the shock of our first sighting had worn off, we understood how revolutionary C1 was going to be. We were believers. We couldn't wait to start developing a campaign for it.

First, however, Steve gave us a challenge: We needed a name for this thing. C1 was on a fast track to production, and the name had to be decided quickly to accommodate the manufacturing and package design process.

"We already have a name we like a lot, but I want you guys to see if you can beat it," said Steve. "The name is 'MacMan.'"

The "i" of My Apple

While that frightening name is banging around in your head, I'd like you to think for a moment about the art of product naming. Because of all the things in this world that cry out for Simplicity, product naming probably contains the most glaring examples of right and wrong.

From some companies, you see names like "iPhone." From others you see names like "Casio G'zOne Commando" or the "Sony DVP SR200P/B" DVD player. (No exaggeration, those are real names.)

Though you might think that the lessons of product naming apply only to companies that create products, that's not true at all. Everyone who communicates, in any organization, would benefit from understanding and applying the principles of good product naming. Maybe it's how you title a report. Or how you theme a conference. In the end, it's all about getting people's attention and making sure they get the feeling you want them to get.

Product naming is the ultimate exercise in Simplicity. It requires one to capture in a single word, possibly two, the essence of a product or company—or in some cases create a personality for it. While Simplicity enjoys a challenge like this, unfortunately so does Complexity. In fact, if you look around at product names, you'll realize that Complexity is doing a fine job of winning this particular war.

Now let us return to the tale of C1. Or should I say, MacMan.

The agency team was heartbroken to learn that Steve had fallen in love with such a disappointing name as "MacMan." Unlike C1 itself, for which our feelings had evolved from shock to love, there could be no love for

"MacMan." Ever. It had so many things wrong with it, we didn't know where to start.

Phil Schiller, Apple's worldwide marketing manager, was in the room, and Steve revealed that "MacMan" was Phil's contribution.

"I think it's sort of reminiscent of Sony," said Steve, referring of course to Sony's legendary Walkman line of personal music players. "But I have to tell you, I don't mind a little rub-off from Sony. They're a famous consumer company, and if MacMan seems like a Sony kind of consumer product, that might be a good thing."

We were surprised to hear Steve's reasoning. It seemed that Apple, more than any company in the world, stood for originality. Having a name that so blatantly echoed another company's style couldn't be the right way to go. We were also disturbed by the "man" part of "MacMan," with its obvious gender bias. And then there was the fact that the name just gave us hives, but we'd need to be a bit more tactful on that one.

This is a common problem dealing with any client. Once they've fallen in love with something you don't like, the only way to really move them off of it is to show them something better. Steve was inviting us to beat "Mac-Man," so it wasn't a terrible problem. Yet.

Before we left the premises, Steve threw out some guidelines for our naming development.

"First of all, you have to know it's a Mac," he said. "So I think it has to have the 'Mac' word in it." This was priority number one, because looks aside, it was a Mac through and through, running all the same software.

"Second, everybody wants to get on the Internet, and this is the easiest way to get there," he said. "It's a no-brainer." An EarthLink installer would be built into the system, so you'd just turn on the computer, fill out the application, and you'd become a full citizen of the Internet—complete with your very own email address. (This was a big deal in those days, I swear.)

Steve had two warnings for us, though—two traps he didn't want us to fall into.

"This is a full-powered Mac, but some people are going to look at it and think it's a toy. So the name shouldn't sound too frivolous," he said.

"There's also a danger people might think it's a portable, because it's got this big handle on the top. But this thing is heavy. That handle is just there to make it easier to move around in the house. So don't make it sound portable," he said.

We scratched our heads at these instructions, given that Steve had just professed love for the name "MacMan." That one name managed to violate both of these instructions simultaneously. "MacMan" sounded both game-like (Pac-Man) and portable (Walkman).

But we'd save that argument for a time when we were equipped with better names. Potential disagreement aside, naming C1 was a terrifically cool opportunity, and the agency team leaped at the chance. A week later, we returned to Cupertino with a portfolio case containing our C1 naming recommendations. We'd gone through a long list of candidates, trimmed it down to five favorites, and created a single poster board for each. Each board presented a name in big, juicy type, along with a short list of bullet points that described its virtues.

Our favorite name was one that I'd come up with early in the process: "iMac." It seemed to solve all the problems at once. It was clearly a Mac. The i conveyed that this was a Mac designed to get you onto the Internet. It was also a perfectly succinct name—just a single letter added to the word "Mac." It didn't sound like a toy and it didn't sound portable.

Using the word "Mac" in the product name was more of a revolution than you might realize. At that time, "Macintosh" had yet to be shortened to a more colloquial "Mac" in the name of any Apple computer. For Simplicity and minimalism, "iMac" seemed to be perfect.

And of course, there was also one other small advantage that came with the name "iMac." It created an interesting foundation upon which Apple could name future consumer products. Maybe, possibly, somehow, sometime, Apple would see fit to create another "i" product?

One by one, I took Steve through our five finalist names. I quickly moved through such also-rans as "MiniMac" (this was long before the Mac mini) and ended with a flourish on "iMac." I made the case that not only was "iMac" concise and easy to remember, but the "i" could stand for other things. There was the obvious association with the Internet, but it could also stand for "individual" and "imagination." Unfortunately, that ending flourish didn't have the desired effect on Steve.

"I hate them all. 'MacMan' is better."

Talk about disheartening. We had expected to be going home heroes, but instead we would be going home to lick our wounds and start up the naming engine once again.

"Now you've only got one week left to come up with a better name, or it's going to be 'MacMan,'" Steve said.

A week later, we'd generated another batch of names. We threw out all the previous names but left "iMac" in the mix, despite the fact that Steve had used the "hate" word. In this presentation, I relied on a philosophy I learned long ago from a wise man in advertising. It was "As long as you've got new ideas to share, you are free to re-present the old one."

Back in Cupertino for presentation number two, I walked Steve through the new names first. After I'd gone through the new list, he still didn't like any. That's when I pulled out "iMac" again and told him we still had a lot of heart for that one. Steve gave it the courtesy of a fresh look.

"Well, I don't hate it this week," he said. "But I still don't love it. Now we've only got a couple days left, and I still think 'MacMan' is the best name we have."

Depressing as that was, there was at least a shred of hope this time around. Steve had said he didn't hate "iMac" anymore. Felt like positive energy to me.

I'd like to say that there was some big turnaround after this point, one moment of glory that had us all high-fiving one another, but there was not. The very next day, while talking to one of my Apple clients, I learned that there was action on the naming front. Steve was making the rounds asking people what they thought of "iMac." He'd had the name silk-screened onto a model to see how it looked.

I never heard another peep about this decision. Steve basically took it and ran. Obviously he liked what he saw when he got the model back, and he must have received positive reactions from his inner circle.

And so, "iMac" it was.

This, of course, says an interesting thing about the way Steve Jobs worked. He had an opinion. A very strong opinion. The kind of opinion that might knock you over and kick you a few times. But that's not to say he wasn't reasonable or wouldn't ultimately change his mind if confronted with heartfelt opinions presented with passion.

This was a key moment for Apple, when its love of Simplicity won the day and set it on a course it follows to this very day. Steve was unrelenting in his desire to give this great product a great name. He appreciated the power of words. In this case, he appreciated the power of a single letter.

And that little letter "i" became one of the most important parts of the Apple brand.

Product Naming for Fun and (Hopefully) Profit

Simplicity can make itself known in many forms: products, strategies, corporate hierarchies, processes, ads, speeches, and a hundred other places. But nowhere is Simplicity found in such a concentrated form as the name of a new product.

You have just a few alphanumeric characters to work with, yet you'd like to communicate something that you could write an essay about. The name will create a unique identity for the product, inject it with a personality, and hopefully contribute to building the company brand.

There are two methods by which a company can create a product name. It can bring in an agency that specializes in such things, which can cost a small fortune, or it can take a whack at it itself.

I'm sure the professionals in the naming field have a thousand reasons why matters of this sort should be "left to the experts." I'm also sure that many big companies simply feel more comfortable trusting outside naming experts to handle the job. This is serious business, and there's way too much riding on it.

If you're a company that specializes in naming products, though, I wouldn't sit by your phone waiting for Apple to call.

Apple doesn't work that way. The names of its revolutionary products were all generated by either Chiat or Apple's product and marketing teams. Given that iMac quickly became the biggest-selling single model in computer history and that iPhone and iPad rocked the world as they did, it's hard to argue with Apple's naming process.

Steve's feeling was that nobody knew Apple's products and plans, or understood the company's culture better, than those inside Apple and Chiat. He wasn't about to pay hundreds of thousands of dollars to an outside expert, probably out of fear that he'd get product names like "Quadra" and "Performa"—computers that were shipped by Apple during his years of exile. Names like those might feel at home on the trunk of a Honda, but they never fit in Steve's world. They reek of traditional corporate values, trying to be simultaneously cool and legally safe.

Because Steve put such a high value on Simplicity in naming, he normally went through many alternatives before making a final choice. You'd think that the name "iPhone" would have been a quick decision due to its obviousness. But many alternate names were developed, partly for the sake of due diligence and partly because there were some legal questions surrounding the name.

Of course, a great name doesn't guarantee a hit product any more than a great education guarantees a perfect life. It simply increases the chances of success. A bad name, however, can indeed become a liability in a product launch. Like everything else in marketing (and life), the goal is to do everything in your power to tilt the odds in your favor. Burdening yourself with a bad product name is one way to hobble a product before it even reaches the shelves.

Having been through the process myself, I can attest to the fact that at some point, after you've filled walls with naming ideas and you've begun to recite thesaurus entries in your sleep, it's easy to convince yourself that the world's supply of good names has been exhausted. (About as likely as the world's musicians running out of original songs to write.) The great name is always there, waiting to be discovered.

Apple makes great use of Common Sense when it names products. It doesn't aim for the spectacular. The iPhone name didn't make people jump up and down, but it made an incredible amount of sense. It came after iMac, iPod, iPhoto, and a host of other "i" products, clearly identifying it as an Apple product. The "phone" part perfectly identified the category it aimed to revolutionize.

Beyond Common Sense, Apple's approach to naming embraces the concept of consistency. Its computers are all Macs, all the time: iMac, Mac Pro, MacBook Air, and MacBook Pro. The "i" identifies Apple's consumer devices, and is always attached to a word that's descriptive of the product or product category. The naming structure across Apple's major product lines is easy for current and potential customers to understand. And every time you say the name of an Apple product, you know it's an Apple product. That's an incredibly powerful concept, as simple as simple gets—but few companies manage to achieve that kind of branding power in their product names.

Over at Dell, product names come from completely unrelated worlds: Inspiron, Vostro, XPS, OptiPlex, Precision, and many more. Every time Dell adds a new product to its portfolio, the name has to fight its way into the vocabulary of the customer. It's true that some of these subbrands have gained recognition over time, but the names bear no relation to one another or to the Dell brand. Things just don't add up for customers as quickly as they do over at apple.com.

The phone manufacturers have a particularly awful time of it, which only serves to make Apple's simple approach stand out even more. Just look at the Motorolas and Nokias of the world. Suffering a perpetual case of product proliferation, these companies have to pay the price when they sit down to name their devices. With literally dozens of models to support, the phone companies drown in a sea of ever-changing names like "Enlighten," "Breakout," "Astound," "Curve," "Citrus," and "Fascinate." These product names tie back to the brand about as well as any random word from the dictionary would.

There are reasons for the naming plight of the big phone makers. They have to strike deals with all the carriers, many of whom demand a unique model name for their stores. If you want them to sell your phones, you have to play by their rules. It's a cycle that the phone makers are powerless to break—unless they're named Apple. By revolutionizing the category Apple created a name that literally sells itself.

Why exactly are so many product names just generic or mediocre? It's because Complexity is deeply embedded in the naming process. A name has to be approved by multiple stakeholders. In most companies it's considered a great victory just to get a name through all the legal obstacles. I've been involved in quite a few naming projects where a name goes out at the end simply because time is up and "this is the best we can get approved."

That kind of talk just isn't tolerated in Cupertino. Apple doesn't settle on product names. Every name needs to be perfect.

Simplicity Is Singularity

Human beings are naturally programmed to identify products by single words. Ask anything more of them and you're bound to be disappointed. People will say, "I'll look it up on my iPhone" but never "I'll look it up on my Apple iPhone."

This, of course, is largely due to the fact that iPhone has achieved powerful brand status on its own. But it's also because Apple has purposefully kept its product portfolio small and manageable—and names its products well. New models of iPhone have come out annually since 2007, but each and every one carries the same name. Modifiers exist to distinguish between models (3GS, 4, 4S, 5, etc.), but such references are used only when conversationally necessary. Again, people will say, "I'll look it up on my iPhone" but rarely "I'll look it up on my iPhone 4." And that's exactly the way it should be, as "iPhone" is the brand and the modifier is for your information only.

Apple pursues a similar singularity in the computer realm. All product lines—iMac, Mac Pro, MacBook Pro, and MacBook Air—retain their familiar names no matter how radically their design may change. Having the same name represent such dramatically different models may cause some complications in record keeping behind the scenes, but Apple is happy to do the extra work if it will make things simpler for its customers.

With several distinct shapes, iPod has its own naming story. Unlike the different models of iPhone, which all have a similar use, the different models of iPod have very different uses. There's iPod touch for an iPhone-like experience with email and apps; iPod nano for full-featured portability; and iPod shuffle—featherweight, screenless and ideal for working out. But even with distinct names for different models, iPod naming is based in Common Sense, with monikers that are descriptive of each model's size or purpose. There are no arcane number-and-letter schemes. There are simply "touch," "nano," and "shuffle." These names themselves have become part of the customers' vocabulary—single words that are easily remembered.

By contrast, the names of most phones sold by Apple's competitors are difficult to remember because there are so many dozens of them, plus the names themselves relate to neither the brand names nor the phones' functions.

Because people are hardwired to gravitate toward a single name, they don't refer to "my HTC Thunderbolt" or "my Motorola Citrus." There is no public research available on this subject, but it would not be surprising if most owners of those models simply referred to their devices as "my phone."

One exception here would be "Droid," which really does resonate with people. It's an excellent name— short, memorable, futuristic, and already familiar given its heritage in *Star Wars* movies. Unfortunately, the Droid name does not accrue benefits to a single phone maker, because the name is actually owned by Lucasfilm and rented out for use by both Motorola and HTC.

Apple doesn't just keep naming simple for the sake of brand-building. It keeps naming simple so it doesn't confuse the hell out of people. At the end of the day, that's what Simplicity does best. With perfect clarity, it tells customers who you are and what you sell.

The One That Got Away

Complexity has a nasty habit of snatching defeat from the jaws of victory.

When I joined the agency working on behalf of Intel, Pentium was the fastest chip around. Intel was spending hundreds of millions of dollars in support of this family of processors, but it had a new vision brewing. It was creating a set of chips especially for mobile computing, incorporating wireless capabilities and the additional technologies required to make mobile magic. All it needed was a name.

At this time, Pentium was a household name. Pentium is a good example of a synthesized name that came to have a well-known meaning due to (a) its ubiquity and (b) Intel's heavy investment in promoting it. Pentium was a branding success—a distinct, powerful subbrand of Intel.

That's what Intel wanted to create for its new mobile technology. But before it could do that, it had to meet two challenges. It needed to come up with a new family name for this technology, and it needed a really good marketing plan.

Common Sense, speaking on behalf of Simplicity, would have required Intel to come up with a name before it came up with a marketing plan. Instead, this cart was going to be sent off in advance of the horse. Intel's debate over the name had been going on for months. So the agency was instructed to come up with a creative marketing plan—but leave a blank space in our ads and materials into which we could plug the name and product logo later.

Compounding this absurdity was the fact that Intel was already sitting on a fabulous name. Just as Apple had created a valuable asset with the "i," someone noticed that Intel had the potential to leverage the style of the Pentium name into something bigger. The "-ium" ending of "Pentium" could be used to create new names in the future, giving all Intel products a family feel. Pentium, sounding like an element off the periodic table, could spawn a line of new "elements"—these elements being the world's most advanced microchips. Going the route of the elements also made sense in that Intel didn't make computers—it made only the most vital ingredient inside of them.

With this in mind, Intel had already come up with a product name for its new mobile platform that not only made Logical Sense (a close relative of Common Sense) but had a little cleverness going for it too. The proposed name was "Mobilium." If this was the work of a naming agency, that agency is to be commended.

Our ad agency saw much potential in "Mobilium." If Intel went in this direction, it would have the opportunity to give its product portfolio a sense of order it had never achieved before. The Mobilium name actually made it into the press as the name of Intel's future mobile platform. However, for reasons never revealed, "Mobilium" was soon relegated to code-name status and taken off the table as a contender for the final product name. As you'll find out later in this book, Intel was a bit gun-shy when it came to legal issues, so chances are that it encountered a thorny trademark issue.

There is an important difference between Intel and Apple when it comes to this sort of thing. Apple faced a legal issue with Cisco concerning the use of the name "iPhone" before that device was ever unveiled. We'll hear more about this in a later chapter, but basically Steve Jobs was so determined to use this name for his world-changing device, he chose to announce it without first securing the legal rights. As a born marketer, Steve was willing to do risky things (and obviously expensive things) when he saw great marketing potential in a name. Whatever problems Intel saw in Mobilium had it running in the opposite direction.

Having killed the Mobilium idea, Intel decided to spend a good sum of cash with a company that specializes in product naming. (The type of company that Steve Jobs would have avoided like the plague.) The name became "Centrino." Intel's corporate identity group went to work and surprised a lot of people by designing a product badge that looked like a sideways butterfly. I mention this only because of a story told to me by a person who was involved with the design. When the original Centrino badge was presented to Intel chairman Andy Grove, he paused for a moment. Fresh from a round of serious medical issues and having become familiar with parts of his internals he would probably rather not, Andy said, "It looks like my prostate." The design was then altered for Andy's benefit.

Graphically speaking and nomenclature-wise, things might have been very different for Intel had it been able to grab the name "Mobilium" rather than "Centrino." But Intel, like many companies, isn't nearly as obsessed as Apple when it comes to Simplicity in naming. To prove that, you need only browse through the product pages on the sites of Dell, HP, Acer and the rest. As you will see in our discussion of iPhone, Apple is a rarity in that it is more than willing to push things to the brink to get the name it believes will deliver the most marketing clout.

But that's why Apple has iMacs, iPhones, and iPads, while Dell has Inspirons, Vostros, and OptiPlexes.

The Joy of Obvious

One of the downsides of Simplicity is that it travels with a curse. That is, sometimes it just seems too easy.

It certainly doesn't seem easy to the person or persons who worked night and day to come up with the simple idea. But to the casual viewer, or even the manager reviewing the idea, it might just look obvious.

Take the name "iPhone," for example. Following the phenomenal success of iPod, the name was so obvious that a thousand news outlets and bloggers were referring to "iPhone" months before Apple ever unveiled it. It was every bit as obvious to Steve Jobs, which was why he wanted to name this product "iPhone" from the start.

As a name, "iPhone" was actually an oversimplification. Steve was extremely clear when he stood onstage for the big reveal: iPhone is three devices in one, he said. It was a phone, an Internet browser, and an iPod. So why "iPhone"? That name described only one third of the device's goodness. You'd think it would have a name more like "iPod," something that wasn't so specific, or a name that at least hinted it was significantly more than a phone. But no—Steve thought "iPhone" was perfect.

It was the obviousness of the name that he found so appealing. If it were called "iPhone," there would be no mistaking how Apple was positioning the product or what industry Apple was about to revolutionize. People would understand the product instantly and that understanding would contribute to the buzz.

Steve had also been around the block a few times in the world of naming. He was well aware that whatever Apple called this device, it would soon be known for its many characteristics, phone included. So he wasn't at all worried that the name might be somewhat limiting, given the many capabilities of the device. Thanks to the buzz created by the news and Apple's own marketing, iPhone would soon stand for much more than "phone."

And so, even though a great many names were paraded before him, Steve stuck with his first love: "iPhone." He thought it was the simplest solution—and if there were any obstacles ahead in securing that name, he was willing to pay the price.

Praying to False Gods

My religious training is very far in the past. But if I recall correctly, there is a commandment that reads, "Thou shalt not lust after thy neighbor's marketing."

It's extraordinary how many companies fall into this trap. I've lost count of the clients I've seen pin their competitors' ads to the wall and openly wish those ads were their own. They want to be someone else, even if that someone has a very different set of circumstances and a very different set of values.

It's fine to have goals or to be inspired by other people's work. But Simplicity requires you to keep your eyes on the road and stay true to your own company's values. It's about authenticity.

Consider the case of Apple's Final Cut Studio, the predecessor of today's Final Cut Pro X. As Final Cut Studio 2 was nearing release, I had the pleasure of being called in to help with a product-naming dilemma.

Final Cut Studio was a collection of high-end video-production tools for editing and special effects. Prior to the release of Final Cut Studio 2, Apple acquired a new addition to this suite of software from another company. This was a "color grading" tool used in Hollywood for very sophisticated color work. Under its previous owner, it had sold for $25,000 per copy, and now Apple was bringing it to the newest version of the Final Cut Studio suite. After much cogitation on a name for this new component, Apple decided to simply call it "Color."

One of those leading the project—we'll call her Jan—was a huge admirer of the way Adobe was selling its video software, Adobe Premiere. At that time, Premiere was available in a number of different "editions," priced according to one's level of need.

What a perfect idea, thought Jan. Apple should do the same. Let's create two editions of Final Cut Studio, regular and premium, with the premium package including the new Color application. She requested packaging design for two products, and a new name for the premium package. If the standard configuration was called Final Cut Studio 2, what would we call the version that included Color?

I became involved in the naming part of the process and shared my suggestions with the package designers. It wasn't my most stellar work, as it contained such gems as "Final Cut Studio 2 Extended Edition" and "Final Cut Studio 2 Platinum Edition." Those names had the air of Adobe about them (or was that the even more stale air of Microsoft?). In truth, there was only one difference between the two products, and that was the presence of Color. So, taking a deep breath, I decided to act upon the obviousness principle. My personal choice was "Final Cut Studio 2, With Color."

Unbeknownst to all of us, though, Steve was in his office polishing the Simple Stick.

At the presentation, a full assortment of package designs, each with its own name, was neatly laid out on the table in front of Steve. The Platinum Edition had a nice shiny platinum stripe across the top. Each of the others had some feature that would help to differentiate it from the standard edition. Jan recapped the mission to set the context for Steve, telling him that this was being done to accommodate the addition of Color to the mix. Steve looked at the boxes, then looked up at the team.

"Put the software in the box," he said.

The group was unsure what he meant. Explanation, please.

"Put Color in the Final Cut Studio box. We sell one product. Period." There was a beat of silence as the group absorbed that. "What next?" he said.

Jan, bless her little heart, felt it was important for Steve to understand why they had done this. She explained that she'd promised the CFO that the software group would create a special edition so it could track and justify the cost of acquiring Color.

"Looks like you made a big mistake," said Steve. And that was it. Meeting over. Final Cut Studio 2 would remain a single box and a single product.

Looking back, I think it was one of those times when Complexity wasn't even trying to be sneaky. It was staring us in the face, yet no one seemed to notice until Steve hit it with the Simple Stick.

By putting all the components of Final Cut Studio into a single box, Apple made things far easier for its customers and far easier for itself. There would be no need to explain on the website the differences between different versions; Apple could simply talk about the big new addition to Final Cut Studio. Nor would there be a need to invest in the design and production of separate packaging and stocking both products in all the Apple Stores. And for Apple's customers, there would be no need to agonize over different versions. They could simply get excited about buying a powerful new product with a brand-new component. Without Color, the upgrades to the new Final Cut Studio 2 would have been minor. Simpler is way, way better.

In this case, it was Jan's overexuberance that was to blame. She was convinced that if she could just find the right name, her product problem would be solved. Unfortunately, her entire quest was inspired by a competitor's values—and not by Apple's rules of Simplicity.

Web Practices for the Clear-Minded

When Apple executives approve the content of apple.com, their goal is to impart information as they stay true to the Apple voice. Apple is warm, welcoming, and smart, and the site is a no-brainer to navigate.

Some who live in digital circles criticize apple.com because it doesn't have a lot of bells and whistles. They say it's just a glorified catalog. Correct on both counts—and that's just the way Steve liked it. He saw apple.com as a place for people to come for more information about Apple's products, period. He wanted it to be interesting and attractive, but he regularly rejected the ideas of those who would expand apple.com in "edgier" directions.

Steve had strict standards for Apple's site regarding what got in and what didn't. He wasn't a big fan of whizzy animations. He believed that such things were "lazy," the mark of a company trying to wow visitors with eye candy rather than substance. He insisted that Apple's site should avoid the frivolous and just make it easy for people to find the information they seek.

Apple's site has matured over the years, and it does incorporate some animation based on the emerging HTML5 standard. These things add some energy to the pages, but Apple steadfastly declines to add tricky digital effects. The result is a site that is consistently rated as one of the most visited sites in the world, and one often praised for its clarity.

Apple lets others experiment with the wild and crazy things. Its goal is to appear as an island of Simplicity in this complicated universe. In that sense, apple.com is the perfect example of what this book is about—using the power of Simplicity to set a company apart.

If you dive deeper, you'll find that some sections of Apple's site aren't totally simple. They have a lot of products to sell and a lot of stories to tell. The important thing is, the pages are designed so they *feel* simple.

Of course, the only thing more important than creating a simple site is making it easy for people to get there. Even here, Steve Jobs made no pretense about his demand for Simplicity. He was even fussy about URLs. At one time, we were sharing a finished commercial with Steve when someone in the room suggested that we use a modified URL at the end of the ad to direct people to a specific Apple page, such as "www.apple.com/specialoffer."

Steve looked stunned that anyone would even suggest such a thing. Thankfully, his turret did not begin to rotate, nor did any verbal beatings ensue. Nonetheless, he very quickly squelched the idea. He just didn't believe that ordinary people would ever remember a specialized URL, and he wanted to make things as simple as possible for them. If an Apple commercial got someone interested in learning more, he felt that this person would instinctively go to apple.com. If we were investing enough money to run a commercial, obviously the Apple home page would prominently feature the relevant link.

With that in mind, look around at all the other commercials you see on TV, or even the ads you see in magazines and newspapers. Look at billboards too. You're bound to see some fairly complicated URLs designed not only to take you to a specific page but also to enable the company to track who's coming from where. Steve didn't believe in making people work harder just so he could collect data about their movements. His most important concern was making things easier for customers. Apple was there to serve them, not the other way around.

He wouldn't like it if a company made him jump through those hoops, and he'd never ask that of anyone else.

Never Underestimate the Power of a Word

Despite the popular notion that Steve Jobs wasn't the world's most considerate person, he did respect the fact that I lived three time zones away in New York. So if it was 1:00 A.M. for me, I could pretty well assume that I would have the rest of the night off. However, if I sent out an email at 1:00 A.M., I would be broadcasting the fact that I was wide awake. I'd have to think long and hard about hitting the "send" button on an email to Steve—for it could easily result in an instant callback and an extended conversation about an ad or anything else he might have in mind.

Steve loved being part of the creative process, and that involved offering up his opinion on every word and image. One night, back in the early days of iMac, I sent one of those late-night emails, and it did provoke an immediate callback from Steve. Despite the time, we spent over an hour going over the copy for a sixteen-page iMac insert soon to go into production.

Of all the different types of interactions I had with Steve, conversations like this were my favorite. It was just the two of us—no distractions or time limits—talking about language. In a certain way, putting together a lengthy piece was a bit like doing a puzzle, and it was both interesting and fun to talk about word choices, implied meanings of words or phrases, and the sometimes microscopic differences between two ways of saying something. Not surprisingly, Steve's main concern was always what the casual reader would take away from it.

That night, we went through our current little epic, page by page and sentence by sentence. We'd rarely get through more than a sentence or two before Steve would make a comment or pose a question. Sometimes we'd talk about big changes; other times we might get into a debate about whether it would be better to use "a" or "the" in a particular sentence. These discussions were never heated. They were just intelligent conversations about the best way to make a point in our marketing. As we got deeper into it, we'd even engage in a bit of horse-trading. If we encountered an issue upon which we could not agree, Steve might say, "Well, you let me have the last one, so I'll let you have this one."

Steve had the sensitivities of an artist and was fanatic about details, just as the legend says. He wasn't debating the use of a single letter because he was controlling, he did this because he thought it was important. For Steve, there was no such thing as an unimportant detail.

As mentioned earlier, when Steve was searching for a product name, he would seek suggestions from inside Apple as well as from his agency team. He demanded that the names conform to the logic of the company's existing naming framework, but he was equally uncompromising about the artistic part: they had to sound good. Even a name as obvious as "iMovie" was debated for weeks, with names flying back and forth by the megabyte.

Apple is unrelenting about sending the message of Simplicity to its customers. It does that with every product it creates—and every word it chooses.

Chapter 7
Think Casual

We were in the agency's rental car about five minutes after leaving Apple, headed to San Jose Airport for the trip back to Los Angeles, when my cell phone rang. It was Steve.

"Look, I don't know who that guy was or why you brought him, but I'm not paying a cent for anything he just did," Steve said, "and I never want to see him at Apple again."

This is what is known in the business as "a bad meeting." Embarrassingly, it was a meeting the agency had spent two weeks preparing for.

The offending party was a planner. We'll call him Hank, so as not to damage his career. In the agency world, planners are those who are paid to represent the consumer's point of view—as opposed to the agency's or the client's point of view. They're the ones who are supposed to figure out what customers are thinking, providing the insights as to what messages might make them more likely to buy.

Planners are supposed to condense all this information into a digestible form that will guide the creative people in developing the most effective work. They are also essential in crafting the marketing strategies that serve as the foundation for the creative work.

Hank was a new hire at the agency. He was a smart guy who had just arrived from one of the most creative agencies in the country, where he worked on the advertising for an account that had achieved iconic status. The aura of his previous job was all over his résumé and he was welcomed with open arms.

It was decided that Hank would get his feet wet by doing a "brand audit" for Apple. He would assess the health of the Apple brand among different demographic groups and ethnicities. His prize was that he'd be able to present his audit to Steve Jobs personally.

Hank had two weeks to do his work, and he dived headfirst into his research. He was eagerly anticipating his meeting with Steve and was determined to do everything in his power to blow him away.

Be careful what you wish for, Hank.

A week before our trip up to Apple, Hank asked if I would take a look at his presentation, since I had a good idea of what type of thing Steve responded to best. I was crammed that day, so we put it off to the next day. Unfortunately, our schedules never got in sync. Day after day, we kept missing each other, and before we knew it, we were flying up to Apple and I had never even seen his presentation. Lee Clow had been working with him, though, so I wasn't concerned. I would just enjoy it as it unfolded, along with Steve.

We got to the Apple boardroom fifteen minutes before meeting time. Hank was carrying one of those awkwardly large portfolio cases containing his presentation materials, and he immediately started to set up. The fact that he had things to set up was the first indication that something was amiss.

Out came a large graph. Followed by a chart with lots of numbers and photos of different kinds of customers. I started to wince, knowing that Steve wasn't a fan of these types of presentations. That's big-company stuff. I felt bad that Hank and I had never been able to connect during the week, because this was starting to look more and more risky—he might well be walking into a death trap.

By the time Hank had emptied his portfolio, there were four large pieces of foam core on the wall, and Hank stood there doing his mental calisthenics. I thought about saying something, but it was way too late for that. So I started doing what any brave advertising guy would do: I made sure I sat outside the line of fire.

When Steve showed up, Lee introduced him to the newest member of our team. He briefly summarized Hank's credentials and explained that he had been working hard on this Apple brand audit—which was something we'd never done before but probably should have. Steve nodded in acceptance, though he seemed more polite than actually interested.

The wall upon which Hank was presenting was actually behind Steve, so Steve swiveled his chair halfway to see the show. His body language was fascinating to watch. He started off at full attention and, minute by minute, sank lower and lower into his chair. He was clearly bored. If it hadn't been for the fact that Lee Clow thought this was a good idea, Steve would have been considerably less polite.

His respect for Lee may have stopped him from shutting down the presentation, but it didn't stop him from heckling. After just a few minutes, he started interrupting to throw out questions. The more it appeared that Steve wasn't buying it, the more nervous Hank became.

A few more minutes into the show, Hank was taking Steve through the different demographic groups he had researched in different cities. "We even went to the ghetto in Harlem and asked the kids on the basketball courts what *they* thought about Apple—"

Steve interrupted yet again. "Why'd you ask them?" he said. "They don't have any money!"

Steve wasn't so much being heartless as just getting more and more annoyed that there was nothing useful in this presentation. Hank fumbled for an answer, and Steve slumped into his seat to the point where he was practically at full recline. He was resting his head in his hand in such a way that he was only peeking at the presentation between two fingers covering his eyes. Now he was just plain appalled.

Lee realized he had to act now or a smart young planner would be psychologically scarred for life.

He interrupted Hank to tell Steve that we wanted to share this research because we thought it was important that we all understand exactly what the Apple brand stands for today, because that might well influence the messages we put out. Steve listened to Lee, but it was clear that he wasn't buying a word of it. In fact, he was getting more and more irritated that we were wasting his time with this.

He looked at Lee with that "I don't get it" expression and took a deep breath.

"Okay, whatever," Steve said. "Let's look at some ads." It was as if Hank had ceased to exist. Hank wasn't finished with his presentation, but Steve had just finished for him. It was pretty clear that Hank's career as Steve's respected partner-in-research had just started and ended, all within the span of twenty minutes.

This was a black mark for the agency, as it had allowed itself to fall into the trap of acting like a typical agency—the kind of agency that Steve didn't like at all. To him, such presentations were the trappings of agencies that dealt in style over substance.

It drove Steve batty to see in twenty slides what could be spoken in three sentences. He valued time way too much for that. He preferred straight talk and raw content to a slick presentation. In fact, a slick presentation would only make him suspect that you were fluffing up the few facts you really had. It meant that you'd devoted valuable time to the wrapping of your idea rather than thinking through the idea itself.

Steve was most comfortable with a table, a whiteboard, and an honest exchange of ideas. He resisted anything that made it feel like relationships were becoming formal, or like Apple might be beginning to display behaviors typical of a big corporation.

He liked the atmosphere in the room to be such that he could put his bare feet up on the table if he felt like it. Which is something he really did do.

Presentations Without Dread

Most business projects begin with one form of briefing or another.

We've all attended briefings that are formal, stiff, and boring, as well as those that are easy to follow and informative. Complexity is perfectly capable of turning a briefing into a type of torture. Simplicity, on the other hand, makes things perfectly clear—and gives participants a true sense of their mission.

During my multiple associations with Apple, I was involved in more than twenty new-product introductions. Some, conducted by the product managers, were designed to get teams working on new product web pages and packaging.

These presentations were brief and interactive. Absent were marketing treatises and complex lists of product attributes. These were just small groups of smart people meeting in a casual atmosphere, receiving a good tour of the product and a clear presentation of its benefits. The product managers were there to answer all of our questions. We'd go away knowing exactly where that product fit in the world and having some fresh incentive to work ourselves to the bone.

The agency often received new product briefings from Steve Jobs himself as part of our regular meetings every other week. Knowing that Steve hated to sit through formal presentations, you might wonder what it was like when Steve was the one doing the presenting.

There was no slide show, no leave-behind, no formalized strategy. It was just a conversation. Sometimes the product was in the room with us, sometimes not. Steve would just share his point of view about why the product existed, how it worked and what set it apart. When necessary, he'd jump to the whiteboard to illustrate his point. In effect, Steve acted as his own slide show. There was no more efficient way to hear about the philosophy behind a product than to hear it from the CEO himself.

Once we absorbed the essence of the product, it was pretty much up to the agency to figure out the most effective way to present it to the world. Steve's confidence in the agency was one of the things that spurred us on. He had hired us because we were smart, and he expected us to prove that time after time. Why should he keep us around if he needed to hold our hands?

Now contrast Apple's methods with the ways other technology companies brief their partners. For many, the more important the project, the more formal a production it becomes. At Dell, Intel, and IBM, a formal project launch could be a megaproduction, sometimes coordinating the efforts of multiple agencies. It was not uncommon for such briefings to be conducted in an auditorium-like room.

When I'm stuck in an exceptionally large meeting and I've run out of things to hold my attention, I sometimes find myself counting the participants to relieve the boredom. My record stands at thirty-two, courtesy of Dell's Consumer group. That was for a summer meeting held to brief various teams on that year's holiday campaign. This briefing consumed an entire day.

Though Dell had the best of intentions, this meeting accomplished little—aside from eating up the time of thirty-two people, many of whom had to travel to attend. It did spawn several focus groups in the Midwest, which required people to travel some more. But in the end, despite the scale of the briefing, Dell decided to do nothing but run some older ads amended with a holiday graphic. The cost of the big briefings and subsequent focus groups, including airfare and hotels, must have been huge.

During all my years working with Apple as both an agency creative director and a consultant, I never attended a formal meeting like this. In fact, I never even attended an overcrowded meeting. There's something in the blood at Dell that requires it—there's something in the DNA of Apple that forbids it.

When you leave a large-scale briefing like that, you're normally burdened with stacks of printouts describing one aspect of the project or another. When you leave a product briefing at Apple, you might have a document that's one or two pages long. Simplicity likes to make a point quickly.

Few people who attend an overblown, hard-to-digest presentation return to their offices eager to set the world on fire. Most prefer to head for the nearest bar. This is not the way to inspire people to greatness. This is simply checking off boxes to make sure every last fact is on the table. It serves the purpose of the presenters, but not the attendees.

I actually don't mean to single out Dell on this topic. This is a recurring issue inside many large companies, as you are likely aware. When you're working with large, unwieldy groups, one begins to feel like a cog in a wheel. When it comes to briefing their partners, most big companies simply follow the template that has produced acceptable results before.

Templates aren't evil in themselves. Internally, Apple does follow a template when it sets up briefings. The difference is, Apple follows a template based on Simplicity. The idea is to give that small group of smart people the information they need to do the highest-quality work.

Death by Formality

When Steve Jobs walked onto a stage, he commanded the world's attention. You'd be reading about it for weeks afterward. So it's no wonder that his presentation style has been the subject of a never-ending stream of books and articles.

However, since most of us don't present in Steve's kind of circumstances—onstage, on camera, in front of five thousand people or more—you might be more concerned about being able to present *to* Steve Jobs. That is, what if someone at Steve's level carved out some precious time on his calendar so you could present an idea to him? How would you use that time?

Steve didn't have a lot of patience. He was supercritical. He'd interrupt you in a heartbeat. If you could successfully present to Steve, I imagine you could successfully present to anybody.

Consideration number one was being respectful of Steve's time. Those who run a big company never have much of it. Those who run two big companies (as Steve did back then) have even less of it. But this plays right into our hands, because Simplicity gains power through brevity. Simplicity is the direct statement, not the meandering rationalization thereof.

Back in the days of NeXT, I learned a lesson in presenting to Steve, one that contradicted everything I'd been taught by my advertising masters up to that point. It changed the way I would approach Steve from that time on, and it changed the way I would present to any client foolish enough to invite me into a project.

The agency team had flown out to share some ideas with Steve for a series of newspaper ads. (Surely you remember newspapers.) As was normal, we had a few minutes in the conference room alone before Steve joined the meeting. That was when I did my job of "setting up" for the conversation. From our large traveling portfolio, I removed the three ads we would be presenting, each mounted on a large piece of black cardboard, creating a beautiful frame effect. In accordance with advertising presentation tradition, I set the ads face down on the table. I didn't really think about it too hard. I just assumed that we'd have a conversation, and at the appropriate time I'd give the setup and flip the ads over one at a time.

Right on time, Steve entered the room and took his place at the table directly in front of the three pieces. I was still new at the job but starting to feel comfortable in my role. Steve had warmed up to the agency and to me. We had a lot of work to do, but it was inspiring and fun.

The meeting started, and the agency's account director started the conversation. Then came my turn. I plunged into the routine I had practiced in my head many times over the last twenty-four hours. I had planned to first recap the strategy, so Steve could appreciate how each ad took a slightly different approach to fulfilling it. I was proud of the work and anxious to share.

I only got about three sentences into my preamble when Steve jumped on me. In the blink of an eye, he went from focused to irritated.

"Just show me the ads!" he said. "Are you going to be sitting next to me to explain things when I read the *Wall Street Journal* in the morning?" He then reached over and flipped up all three of the boards. He looked at them for a moment, absorbing their content without my voiced narration.

Steve was fully aware of what we were working on. He knew what he wanted those ads to accomplish. We probably didn't need to say a word before we flipped them over, and then we simply could have debated which was better and why.

What Steve didn't need at that point was a formal presentation. In effect, he was saying, "Please stop being ad agency guys and just talk to me."

Simplicity is in a hurry. It wants to cut to the chase and concentrate on the important stuff. No insult to you and all the time you've spent preparing that convincing speech, but much of what you're about to say is likely superfluous. Many people incorrectly assume that by increasing the word count they will demonstrate their smarts, when the opposite is almost always closer to reality. Those who know how to communicate with brevity are the ones who come across as smarter and are more appreciated by executives who value their time.

To Steve, the meeting we started to have was something that happens when big companies deal with big agencies. The setup part came across as a form of manipulation. He wanted to judge our ideas on their merits, not on our opinion of how he should react. The more formal the presentation, the more suspicious Steve seemed to get.

There's a thin line between leading clients to a conclusion and treating them like idiots. There was probably a bit of that in Steve's reaction to "being led" as well. The best approach with Steve was to just lay the facts on the table and start the discussion. That was the time to express your opinion and push for the conclusion you believed in.

In many ways, a formal presentation creates a barrier. Just because it ends with "Any questions?" does not mean it promotes conversation. At the end of the day, most businesses come down to relationships. A less formal presentation with honest debate is the way to strengthen your relationships— and get better results.

The informality of Steve's conference room style was based on the fact that he considered most meetings to be brainstorming sessions. Even if you brought finished work to the meeting to share, it would be discussed and dissected before you left the room. The only time Steve believed in making a formal presentation was when he was onstage unveiling a new Apple product.

Apple's launch events were painstakingly choreographed and rehearsed to the nanosecond. There was a backup plan for everything that might possibly go wrong. But even in an onstage production so perfectly planned, the informal Steve could easily be seen.

If you were to look at a slide show that accompanied one of Steve's onstage presentations without Steve's persona to walk you through it, you'd be surprised how utterly simple it is. It's straightforward to a fault. Absolutely, Steve's purpose was to steer the audience toward the conclusion he wished, but he did so in the most direct way. In fact, in many ways he followed the traditional presentation playbook: Lay out the agenda, lay out the facts for each topic, then summarize each topic before moving on to the next. At the end of the show, he'd summarize the high points of the entire show all over again. If he had a thought he wanted you to remember, he'd repeat it. Over and over.

Steve was relentless about rehearsing and tweaking his big product unveilings for days and weeks, to make sure the world saw what he wanted it to see. In that sense, these events were formal. However, Steve wasn't a polished presenter in the traditional sense. He didn't stand erect, speak slowly, and enunciate like he'd just come from presentation class. He spoke more like a passionate twenty-year-old with the wisdom of a fifty-year-old. What made people relate to him was that despite all the rehearsing (and to some degree, because of it), he still came across more like the guy in the conference room than the CEO onstage.

This was the same Steve who communicated to his employees and partners. Never once did I hear him ask the agency for a formal presentation—just our best thinking.

Chapter 8
Think Human

By the time he reached his forties, Steve had pretty much experienced the full range of emotions one could feel when working with a new computer. At various times, he'd been amazed, proud, angry, fascinated, frustrated, inspired, and incensed.

So on one particular late-night phone call, I was surprised to hear Steve become quiet and reflective. "This was the first time a computer made me cry," he said.

Just a few hours earlier, he had sat down in front of a prototype iMac and tried his hand at iMovie—a new product he'd be unveiling to the world in the near future. His experience was transformative. He imported some video of his kids from his camcorder, grabbed the best clips, added transitions and titles, chose a great sound track, and created a movie that touched his heart.

He told me that when he showed it to his wife, they both got tears in their eyes. He thought this was one of the best products Apple had ever made. He marveled at the Simplicity of it.

To properly appreciate the moment, you'll have to transport yourself back to 1999. In those days, there was no YouTube, yet camcorders had already become a hot consumer product. While many people were filling boxes with videocassettes from their camcorders, few had a clue how to turn all that video into classic movies they could share with friends, relatives, and unsuspecting visitors.

iMovie was going to change that. Steve thought it was amazing that technology could have this kind of emotional effect, and he shared his experience because he thought it would be cool if we could capture that kind of emotion in the iMovie ads we were about to produce.

As a direct result of this call, the agency conceived an ad that was very much like Steve's story. We called it *Crying Man*, because for the better part of thirty seconds, we would see only a man dabbing tears from his eyes as he watched something out of frame. We'd hear the sound track of his movie and see that the man was spellbound, but not until the end would we see that he was watching a movie about his beautiful young daughter—something he'd created himself on his new iMac. It doesn't get any more emotional than *that*, we thought.

After much casting, we found a father type who was young, good-looking, and capable of crying buckets on cue. We shot the commercial. But only in editing did we realize our terrible mistake. Without any kind of backstory established, the ad seemed to tell the story of a grieving dad devastated by the loss of his daughter, reliving her memory on video. Not exactly the uplifting message we'd planned.

Fortunately, we quickly found a way to demonstrate iMovie without making it feel like there was a funeral involved. We used a fun movie created by an Apple VP featuring his kids jumping up and down on a bed to the tune of Bob Dylan's "Forever Young." With this spot, Apple became the first advertiser in history to use a genuine Dylan recording. This was another emotional moment for Steve, as Dylan's music had helped shape his own life.

The iMovie project revealed a part of Steve that would soon become a lot more visible. He'd always been proud of Apple's ability to connect with people, but now the company was going places where it would be connecting on a more emotional level. Looking back, iMovie was just a baby step in that direction. In the coming years, Apple would turn emotional connection into an art form by bringing customers closer to their music, photos, and movies, and closer to their family and friends. It would even bring them closer to the technology itself, using touch and voice.

Revolution by revolution, Apple would prove that the most powerful form of Simplicity is that which connects directly to our humanity.

Technology with Feeling

From the beginning, Apple has succeeded because it makes products that reflect human values. (We'll conveniently overlook the bleak times during Steve's absence when the company began to lose sight of its own values.) Back when PCs required us to think like machines, Macintosh changed everything by letting us think like people. It was simpler.

But in the last decade in particular, Apple's brand of Simplicity has become increasingly attuned to our humanity. By appealing to our emotions, our love of art and design, Apple's inventions have gone far beyond mere functionality to become objects of lust. So much so that grown adults will actually stand in line for half a day to get them.

As Apple's first handheld consumer device (let's not count Newton), iPod was the product that helped Apple turn this corner.

It entered a category that already offered a number of choices in music players. Complexity reigned, with every device working by its own rules. There was no heavyweight player in this category, only a bunch of companies scrambling to carve out a niche. Never having seen Apple lacking for confidence, I imagine it surveyed this scene and felt much like Charlton Heston's character did in the opening minutes of *Planet of the Apes*, when he looked out over a tribe of primitive humans and said, "If that's the best there is around here, in six months we'll be running this planet."

Apple believed that what the music player category needed most was Simplicity, and whichever company delivered it would soon be "running this planet." It turned out that one key insight allowed Apple to leap ahead of the other companies. Steve explained in a 2006 *Newsweek* interview:

> *We had the hardware expertise, the industrial design expertise, and the software expertise, including iTunes. One of the biggest insights we [had] was that we decided not to try to manage your music library on the iPod, but to manage it in iTunes. Other companies tried to do everything on the device itself and made it so complicated that it was useless.*

By removing the Complexity, Apple created a device that brought people closer to their music. It was a device that appealed on human terms, removing the barrier of technology.

In creating iPod, Apple gained technical skills in miniaturization and interface design that opened the doors for more human-centric devices to come. With its touch screen and intuitive interface, iPhone was worlds apart from BlackBerry—again, because it seemed to treat us like people instead of fellow machines. And, of course, iPad disrupted the computer marketplace in much the same way.

But the most human of all Apple technologies was still to come. With Siri, the intelligent assistant that debuted on iPhone 4S, Apple has moved beyond the touch screen, adding even more humanity to its products. Siri responds to the human voice, intelligently parsing words to execute a series of actions. Ask Siri if you need an umbrella today, and she cheerfully figures out your location, gets the weather report, and offers a suggestion. Clearly this is the future of our relationship with technology, from phones to TVs to computers. As predicted in so many sci-fi films, we will soon have a conversational relationship with our technology. Let's just hope it works out a little better than HAL in *2001: A Space Odyssey*.

The genius of Apple is that it often sees human potential where other companies do not, and it has the design and engineering skill to bring its vision to life. Sometimes, as happened with iPod and the music player market, Apple doesn't actually invent the idea from scratch. The concept may already exist but be missing only one thing: Simplicity. And that makes all the difference in the world.

Steve Jobs, Card-Carrying Human

If Steve Jobs believed so deeply in the power of Simplicity, and Simplicity is such an important part of being human, why was he such a maniacal tyrant?

Well, maniacal tyranny is in the eye of the beholder. No one denies that Steve was incredibly demanding, relentlessly tough, and, in certain moments of passion, outright scary. His bottom line was that the ship had to be moving forward every day. If you weren't helping, that's when you got in trouble.

But there were actually two Steves—the merciless, controlling, unrelenting Steve and the inspiring, charming, and deeply human Steve. It was this combination that made him so fascinating, and it's what made so many people devote their energy, and much of their lives, to his vision.

Though he didn't suffer fools gladly, Steve put his faith in people to solve impossible problems and create amazing computers and devices. His job was to create the conditions in which that could happen. He did that by driving people to reach their potential and by promoting collaboration, which he believed was a key part of creative thinking.

In building Pixar's new home, Steve had it designed so people would frequently gather in common space, adding a spontaneous aspect to collaboration. He elaborated in a 2004 *BusinessWeek* interview:

> *Process makes you more efficient. But innovation comes from people meeting up in the hallways or calling each other at 10:30 at night with a new idea, or because they realized something that shoots holes in how we've been thinking about a problem. It's ad hoc meetings of six people called by someone who thinks he has figured out the coolest new thing ever and who wants to know what other people think of his idea.*

Steve believed in those "happy accidents," the random meetings that might result in an exchange of ideas or start conversations between people who wouldn't normally interact.

Though his outbursts were legendary, Steve could also be incredibly supportive. In fact, some of his praise seemed to be piped in directly from his reality distortion field: "This is the greatest launch in the history of computers." Maybe you knew that it wasn't really true, but the fact that he was distorting reality just for you created a warm and fuzzy feeling.

It would have been offensive if Steve had asked us to work harder than he did. But he didn't. He only asked us to work exactly as hard as he did. I have no idea how he did it, but in the years following his return to Apple he would be CEO of Apple three days a week, CEO of Pixar two days a week, and CEO of both on weekends. Yet there were still times when he'd be unavailable because he'd promised his family he'd take them to a movie.

(Steve would later claim to his biographer Walter Isaacson that his cancer began as a result of his extreme exhaustion from working both jobs. Isaacson correctly points out that there is no evidence cancer can be caused by exhaustion or lowered immune system.)

But if you're really looking for evidence of Steve's humanity, you only have to look at what he created. When you see his innovations in use at hospitals, art studios, universities, and preschools, you know exactly what made him tick.

Here's to the Crazy One (Steve)

Earlier, I described the *Think different* campaign as Steve's first foray into advertising after he returned to Apple in 1997. The commercial we created to launch the campaign, entitled *The Crazy Ones*, was meant to express Apple's philosophy.

After we created this commercial, Chiat's chief, Lee Clow, had the idea that there was only one person in the world who could read it like it came from the heart—that was Steve himself. It was a pretty great idea, but we had no idea how it would sound until we tried it. So one day I dutifully traveled up to Cupertino, sound engineer in tow, just so we could get Steve's read. We set up in the Apple auditorium. When Steve showed up, he made it clear that (a) he really didn't think this was a good idea and (b) he was busy, so he was only going to read it once. I considered it a major victory that I was able to get three takes out of him before he said, "I'm finished" and walked out. During that late night when we put the final touches on this commercial, we made a valiant effort to persuade Steve that his voice would work best, but he resisted. He thought the fact that he was reading the script would create controversy and distract people from the message of the ad, which he thought was so important.

Though he didn't fancy himself as the voice, Steve had a major passion for *The Crazy Ones*. He seemed to get goose bumps from it. He played it at key events, even some ten years after it first ran. He felt that it perfectly captured the spirit of the company he'd built.

Only years later, now that we can look back and more fully appreciate Steve's role in revolutionizing computers, music, movies, and phones, does it become clear that the script for this ad wasn't just describing Apple, it was describing Steve himself:

Here's to the crazy ones.
The misfits.
The rebels.
The troublemakers.
The round pegs in the square holes.
The ones who see things differently.
They're not fond of rules.
And they have no respect for the status quo.
You can quote them,
disagree with them,
glorify or vilify them.
About the only thing you can't do is ignore them.
Because they change things.
They push the human race forward.

And while some may see them as the crazy ones,
we see genius.
Because the people who are crazy enough
to think they can change the world . . .
are the ones who do.

After Steve passed away, when Apple staged a celebration of his life at its Cupertino headquarters, CEO Tim Cook played the audio recording of Steve reading the script for *The Crazy Ones*. Steve really did do a beautiful job of it, quite distinct from the Richard Dreyfuss version. (He made his recording before he ever heard Dreyfuss's.) Over a decade after it was created, Steve's read has finally made it out of the Chiat vault and onto YouTube. If you haven't heard it already, it's well worth seeking out.

A widely circulated rumor about this commercial is that it was written by Steve, or that he wrote a substantial part of it. In truth, he inspired the ad in many ways, he was totally involved with it from start to finish, and he had lots of valuable input. And as a writer he did contribute this line: "They push the human race forward."

It's interesting, because if you were to look for the one line in this ad most descriptive of Steve's life, I believe that would be it. Pushing the human race forward is far more important than merely inventing cool stuff. While Steve's vision was delivered revolution by revolution, clearly his sights were set higher. He saw Apple creating products that would literally change the world for the better.

By making advanced technology simpler, Steve truly did push the human race forward.

The Further Humanization of Steve

We are all shaped by the experiences of our lives. We can't help but change when we experience profoundly moving events. By most accounts, Steve started out brash and abrasive, then grew up to be . . . brash and abrasive. But that's not to say he wasn't a changed man.

Though he was always intensely driven and highly competitive, three events in Steve's life ensured that he would maintain perspective and not lose sight of his humanity.

The first came in 1985, when he was forced out of Apple. The story is old enough that many don't remember it correctly or may never have known it in the first place. It's water under the bridge from a historical perspective, but being forced to leave the company he created was something that really affected Steve. How could it not?

Imagine being in Steve's shoes. With his partner, Steve Wozniak, he started the company that popularized the personal computer. He built it into a multimillion-dollar corporation, then revolutionized computers again with Macintosh—changing the way all computers would work in the future. As the company grew, he recognized that he needed a big-business brain to run the nuts and bolts of the operation while he guided future product development. He personally recruited John Sculley, who ended up driving him out of the company he had built, the company in which he had invested all his energy and emotion.

This was Steve's first major humbling experience, and it was a profound one. It brought him face-to-face with the fact that he wasn't invulnerable. Or infallible. He had to absorb the fact that when faced with the choice, his own board of directors preferred to see him leave.

A *Rolling Stone* article in 1994 included a quote from an unnamed colleague who made this observation about Steve being driven from Apple:

Remember, this is a guy who never believed any of the rules applied to him. Now, I think he's finally realized that he's mortal, just like the rest of us.

Not only did Steve have to suffer a public humiliation, he had to watch Apple flounder over the years, sinking deeper into a black hole as a series of CEOs tried in vain to restore the magic. If this experience wasn't bad enough, Steve then moved directly to life-changing event number two.

Unlike his lightning-quick humbling at Apple, his humbling-to-come would take place over a period of eleven years.

Out of Apple, Steve started a new computer company—making very sure he would retain the majority share forever. He called it NeXT.

The story of how he got that name has actually never been told. One of Steve's oldest friends and business associates was Tom Suiter, a San Francisco–area designer. When Steve was starting his new company, he called Tom to tell him he'd come up with a name for it. He would call it "Two"—because it was his second company. Tom wasn't impressed. "But then everybody's going to ask what happened to the first company," he said. To which Steve replied, "Well, that's why I'm calling you. Can you think of anything better?"

Shortly afterward, Tom attended a speech by Bill Gates in Seattle. He was struck by the number of times Gates used the word "next" as he described new technologies being developed by Microsoft. That word kept echoing in his head. The more he thought about it, the more right it seemed. A few days later Tom called Steve and said, "I think I have the name for your new company. It's 'Next.'" There was a long pause while Steve soaked it in. And then came the enthusiastic "I love it!"

It's ironic that a speech by Bill Gates was actually the spark for the naming of NeXT. Even more amazing, neither Steve nor Bill were ever aware of it. (And whoever would have thought that Gates would, however indirectly, be responsible for such a burst of Simplicity.)

The name NeXT really was perfect in that it was simultaneously autobiographical (Steve's next adventure after Apple) and visionary (devoted to developing the next great computer). At NeXT, Steve had to start over from scratch. He had to hire a founding team, create a business plan, find partners to help fund it, and hire/inspire a whole new set of employees. And, of course, he'd have to create a product people would want to buy.

Unlike Apple, NeXT's products weren't for consumers. This time around, Steve was targeting the corporate world. Also unlike Apple, NeXT did not rocket out of the starting gate. Many experts wondered if the world really needed a new kind of computer, and so did many of the customers Steve was trying to reach.

So NeXT was a constant struggle. There were moments of brilliance, and Steve performed well as superstar, showman, and salesman—but this was very much an uphill battle. Three years into it, Steve introduced the company's first product. The NeXT Computer was a sleek, black twelve-inch cube filled with computing goodness, representing several major leaps forward for the industry. Steve personally helped formulate the headline that launched the NeXT Computer. Over a gorgeous shot of the cube, display, and printer were these words:

In the 90s, we'll probably see only ten real breakthroughs in computers. Here are seven of them.

Steve tried to spin his new story to the best of his ability, targeting journalists, analysts, and potential IT customers. This was Steve doing his best Pied Piper routine.

However, his reality distortion field wasn't working so well here. After several years of trying, Steve had to give up on the computer and focus on NeXT's strength: its innovative software called NeXTSTEP. He created a new version of NeXTSTEP that would run on standard Intel-powered PCs and tried to sell his technology that way. But the going got tougher and NeXT just didn't generate a lot of magic. It had to have weighed on his ego.

In Steve's absence, Apple hadn't created any magic either. Things were looking bleaker and bleaker down in Cupertino. The Mac operating system had gotten extremely long in the tooth, and Apple desperately needed a new OS if it was to counter the advances of Microsoft Windows and establish a solid foundation for its future. Having failed for a number of years in its own efforts to create a next-generation OS, Apple became convinced (largely because of Steve's pushing) that it could solve its problems by acquiring NeXTSTEP. Apple purchased NeXT in 1996 for $429 million and 1.5 million shares of Apple stock—and got Steve as "adviser" to CEO Gil Amelio in the deal.

Ironically, both of these humbling experiences—being ejected from Apple and going nowhere for all those years with NeXT—turned out to create the best possible future for both Steve and Apple.

Steve matured at the University of NeXT. He got better at running a business. He learned the economics of innovation. He got really good at attracting partners and building alliances. He got better at inspiring his employees. He learned some humility by being humbled so publicly. Best of all, he created the software that would become the foundation of Apple technology—for desktops and mobile devices—for years to come.

All those years with NeXT made Steve a better businessman, a better leader, and, having lived through the hardship, a better human being.

Delivering the commencement speech at Stanford on June 12, 2005, Steve addressed this very topic:

I didn't see it then, but it turned out that getting fired from Apple was the best thing that could have ever happened to me. The heaviness of being successful was replaced by the lightness of being a beginner again, less sure about everything. It freed me to enter one of the most creative periods of my life. . . .

I'm pretty sure none of this would have happened if I hadn't been fired from Apple. It was awful-tasting medicine, but I guess the patient needed it. Sometimes life hits you in the head with a brick.

Before Steve would utter these words publicly, however, he was humbled for a third time—and this would have the most profound effect on Steve's being. It was his own brush with mortality.

There's no more sobering thing in life than the realization that your life is ending. When he was first diagnosed with pancreatic cancer in 2004, Steve was told it was time to "get his affairs in order," because his cancer was incurable. The end would come quickly.

Here was Steve, husband, father, and guiding spirit of Apple, coming to grips with the fact that his time was nearing an end. In that Stanford speech, Steve gave the world a rare glimpse into one of the most deeply personal moments in his life. Though the news was terrible, he was able to talk about it objectively and point out its positive effects:

Remembering that I'll be dead soon is the most important tool I've ever encountered to help me make the big choices in life. Because almost everything—all external expectations, all pride, all fear of embarrassment or failure—these things just fall away in the face of death, leaving only what is truly important. Remembering that you are going to die is the best way I know to avoid the trap of thinking you have something to lose. You are already naked. There is no reason not to follow your heart. . . .

No one wants to die. Even people who want to go to heaven don't want to die to get there. And yet death is the destination we all share. No one has ever escaped it. And that is as it should be, because death is very likely the single best invention of life. It is life's change agent. It clears out the old to make way for the new.

It turned out that Steve's condition when first diagnosed wasn't fatal after all. He had hope. But it's impossible to live through something like this without feeling its impact for the rest of your life. As circumstances would play out, he never did manage to regain his full health and spent a number of years leading Apple with the full realization that he had only a limited time remaining.

His experiences at Apple and NeXT were humbling in the sense that his ego was humbled. His experience dealing with the possibility of death was humbling in a far more profound way. He had to confront the knowledge that we're all mortal and we need to think carefully about what we contribute in the time we have. Many years earlier, Steve had expressed the desire to "put a dent in the universe." Surely his health issues only reinvigorated his desire to do so.

One can't have a deep feeling for Simplicity without being able to appreciate human values and understand what drives human behavior. You can see Steve's humanity, and his devotion to the idea of empowering humanity, throughout his time at Apple. He put computing power in the hands of ordinary people with the Apple II. With Macintosh, he humanized computing by replacing arcane commands with the graphical "point-and-click" interface. With iPad, he made computing power accessible to all ages and disciplines, enhancing the way we live, learn, work, play, and discover.

Steve's professional and life experiences, bitter as they sometimes were, served to make him even more sensitive to people's hopes and dreams. Though he was criticized on a personal level by those who disagreed with his vision, Steve did a very good job of being human.

Technology Not Spoken Here

The technology that drives Apple devices is incredibly complex. One with technical expertise could write dissertations describing how these "simple" devices do what they do.

But Apple never will. It prefers to speak in more human terms.

Apple didn't describe the original iPod as a 6.5-ounce music player with a five-gigabyte drive. It simply said, "1,000 songs in your pocket." This is the way human beings communicate, so this is the way Apple communicates.

Human-speak is a hallmark of Simplicity. It's the recognition that the best way to connect with people is to put things in human terms and use the words that people use in everyday conversation.

This way of speaking is front and center in all Apple communications and it has been since the company was founded. Apple makes it look effortless, and a great many marketers set out to behave similarly—but few of them succeed.

Why? Because what looks so effortless requires a lot of hard work. Once again, it's the curse of Simplicity—it looks deceptively simple. So many companies look at what Apple does and assume they can just snap their fingers to take advantage of the power of Simplicity themselves. They may ask for a new ad campaign, create an inspiring manifesto, call company meetings, hand out T-shirts, maybe even put a new sign up in the conference rooms—and then . . . nothing really changes.

Complexity is far too clever to allow a company to attain Simplicity through proclamation. If the love of Simplicity isn't instilled into its people and burned into its products, if people aren't rewarded for acts of bravery in support of Simplicity, the concept will come and go like Human Resources' annual benefits meeting.

So how does Apple do it? How does it keep its voice constant, speaking the language of human beings year after year? Doesn't it face the same obstacles all companies face?

Apple's big advantage is that it didn't establish its voice yesterday. It's one of those "overnight sensations" thirty years in the making. It has consistently communicated in a human, nontechnical way for so long, it's burned into the system. People expect Apple to be human and they reward Apple for being human. Companies who wish to connect with people in a more Apple-like way can create initiatives that point them in the right direction, but remember, Simplicity is an all-or-nothing proposition. If the company's culture doesn't support this type of behavior, it will never be more than window dressing.

As someone who has sat in countless marketing meetings inside IBM, Intel, and Dell, I can report one amazing fact. In the majority of meetings I attended in those places, a positive reference to Apple's communications came up at least once. Apple is the gold standard by which many companies judge clarity and consistency of message.

With similar frequency, I hear the same types of references from other clients, even those outside of technology. Former colleagues tell me that it's become commonplace for their clients to demand that their agency try something that's "more like Apple."

Though most don't realize it, what they're really asking for is a healthy dose of Simplicity. Most will never achieve it because their goal is a quick fix and not a meaningful change. And as we know, Simplicity is more about commitment than indulgence.

There is also the unfortunate reality that many companies are Simplicity resistant. Their corporate cultures and institutionalized processes prevent them from achieving Simplicity, or they are staffed by people who can never muster more than a surface commitment to it. Even when they aim toward Simplicity, these companies tend to fall back on what's comfortable. Either that or they reserve a place at the table for Complexity's old friend, Compromise. Before you know it, that "new" approach starts feeling an awful lot like the old approach—and all the ones that came before.

It's only natural for companies to be influenced by past behaviors. In Apple's case, that's a very good thing. It's called consistency. The challenge to any company seeking to embrace Simplicity is being consistent with its new values long enough so they become part of the culture. Otherwise, Simplicity ends up being a suit that's only worn at special events—not exactly a DNA changer.

Apple's history of human-speak dates back to a time when its products weren't all that simple. In 1977 the Apple II became the company's first hit, the computer that made Apple famous. In those days, the idea of a "personal computer" was way out there. An IBM Selectric typewriter was the principal object of envy for office workers who had any awareness of technology.

Interestingly, the brochure Apple created to introduce the Apple II in 1977 bore the headline "Simplicity is the ultimate sophistication." At the bottom of the page, in the same size type, came the second half of the line: "Introducing Apple II, the personal computer."

Most Mac users have an allergic reaction to the term "PC," but back then that's what Apple called its own products. In fact, at one time the company's theme line was "The most personal computer."

Before Apple came along, people had no concept that a computer would ever let them share photos, stay connected with friends, listen to music, or do any of the things we take for granted today. Most computers were for doing accounting work in big companies. The idea of having one at home was either absurd or frightening.

It took a company that understood what makes people tick to convince them that they might actually enjoy having a computer. Apple's solution then was as people-centric as its solutions are today.

One of the boldest things Apple did to speak to its fellow human beings was create a multipage foldout insert for major magazines that became one of Apple's early "classics." This is how bold statements were made before there was an Internet.

Apple's task wasn't to tell the world why its computer was better than anyone else's (there weren't any others) or to brag about its specifications (grotesquely puny by today's standards). It had to start with the basics—it had to convince people a computer could open new doors for them. The magazine insert was designed to tackle that problem head-on. The headline asked, "Will someone please tell me exactly what a personal computer can do?" The cover opened to reveal four full pages side by side, stuffed to the gills with a list of a hundred things you could do. Many of these items were brought to life with a colorful and/or fanciful illustration—creating a seductive array of uses for the reader to explore.

More than an eyeful, this ad was a headful—offering up things people had never imagined doing with a computer, from playing games to writing a novel, from learning math to running a business. It was engaging and enlightening and written in a way that made you want to read more. It was a human articulation of a technological breakthrough. Though the volume of information was large, the concept was simple. Because it spoke our language, the ad was fantastically successful. (This insert was created by Steve Hayden—the very man who would later be responsible for creating the *1984* commercial that launched Macintosh.)

This human way of speaking became Apple's trademark at the very beginning. Despite the fact that Apple's products were pure technology—assemblages of circuit boards, buttons, and enclosures—Apple made it clear that they were made for ordinary people who wanted to do extraordinary things. It took something that was inherently complicated and turned it into something that was wonderfully simple.

Of course, simple is relative. If you were to look at those early Apple computers today, they'd seem ridiculously complicated. No mouse, no graphics, just a command-line interface—very much like the PCs with which Macintosh would later battle.

But even at the dawn of the personal computer, Apple understood the role that humanity would play in technology—and the importance of using Simplicity to communicate it.

Say No to Arrogance

Apple takes great pride in being the most "human" technology company.

But while many see positive human qualities in Apple, there are detractors who see a human failing. They believe Apple operates with a disturbing arrogance.

You can trace that perception all the way back to the first Macintosh in 1984. Apple was everyone's friend when it first put computing power into the hands of ordinary people with the Apple II. But with Macintosh, it was pushing its way into a business world dominated by PCs. Many in the establishment saw Macintosh as a toy, with its childish graphics and silly "mouse."

Apple didn't exactly quell those perceptions of arrogance with the *1984* Super Bowl ad, which depicted IBM as Big Brother, and the 1985 Super Bowl ad, *Lemmings*, which insulted the very customers it was trying to reach—showing a line of businesspeople walking single file off a cliff. It didn't matter that PCs ultimately embraced the graphical interface and mouse. The cultural divide would last for decades.

Today Apple's detractors see a different kind of arrogance. They rail against Apple's unbending desire to control all aspects of the mobile experience—the hardware, the system software, what apps you buy and where you buy them. And to be fair, there have been times when Apple has helped fan the flames of arrogance itself—like when Steve Jobs answered a customer who complained via email that his grip on the iPhone 4 was causing a signal loss by saying, "Just avoid holding it in that way."

In one sense, Apple doesn't give a hoot about those who see arrogance. They're not Apple customers and aren't likely to be. Apple does care deeply about the people who share its values—and the number of those people has been rising dramatically in recent years, vindicating Apple's business philosophy.

However, when Apple speaks to the world through its marketing, the question does arise: How can it aggressively compete without feeding the perception of arrogance?

With its Mac advertising, Apple tried at several points to make inroads against PCs. Having far less than a 10 percent market share for most of the last fifteen years, there was certainly room to grow. The *Switchers* TV campaign that ran in 2002 and 2003, featuring colorful stories from people who had made the switch from PCs, got a lot of notoriety. Unfortunately, it didn't translate to a lot of switching.

But in 2006, riding a wave of consumer interest powered by the revolution of iPod, Apple tried to win over PC users again. This time it succeeded beyond its wildest dreams.

The *Mac vs. PC* campaign became a cultural phenomenon—sixty-six ads that ran over a period of four years—sparking more interest and attention than any campaign in Apple's history. Rarely does a campaign in any category produce so many popular spots over such a long period of time.

It hit a nerve because Chiat came up with a unique format that allowed Apple to turn a discussion of the Mac's most important attributes into entertainment. The ads presented Mac and PC as real people, each with a unique personality perfectly matched to the platform it represented. Justin Long played the down-to-earth, "it just works" Mac, while John Hodgman played the part of PC, doing his best to project an air of confidence despite the evidence stacked against him.

Each commercial was another episode in the long-running relationship between the two, and their clever back-and-forth allowed them to highlight their differences. It is important to note that the *Mac vs. PC* campaign was a good-natured take on the rivalry, so even when Apple delivered a particularly devastating blow against the PC world, it came off as a friendly jab—but viewers got the meaning.

Being competitive without being arrogant is a difficult thing. Launching sixty-six scathing attacks upon your archcompetitor while still being lovable is a really, *really* difficult thing. But that's what *Mac vs. PC* managed to do. Thanks to its wit, Apple seemed perfectly well behaved even as it ripped PCs to the core.

You'd think that such a brilliant advertising idea would have been green-lighted from the start. In truth, the campaign had shaky beginnings, as Steve rejected many of Chiat's scripts over the course of several meetings. Refusing to give up on their idea, the Chiat team decided that the best thing to do was to go out and shoot some real ads using the proposed actors. They spent an intense weekend doing just that and shared the ads with Steve on Monday. Seeing them on the screen instead of on paper, he loved them.

The result was a campaign that featured the most competitive ads ever produced by Apple—high on the aggression meter and low on the arrogance meter.

Babies and Puppies Not Required

Given that Simplicity and humanity are longtime partners, let's bust up one of the greatest myths about what makes a company "human."

If you've served more than a few years on the marketing front, you've probably been in many meetings where a client demanded more humanity in its ads. Most of the time, when clients ask for humanity, they're really asking to see images of people. After all, you can't be human unless you show images of human beings, right?

Though it's excruciatingly obvious that humanity and humans go together, the truth is that they can also stand apart. It's a question of how imaginative you'd like to be and what kind of picture you choose to paint. What determines the humanity in a company's messages is *tone*—which is the combined effect of the words and images it chooses to use.

A human presence in imagery is absolutely one way to add humanity, but words can be every bit as human. When you tell a coworker that you cried at your daughter's school play last night, you don't need to produce photographic evidence. The way you tell the story contains all the emotion.

Historically, communicating with a human tone has been one of Apple's greatest skills. It didn't need to show a mom sitting at the computer with a baby on her lap to prove it was a human company. One could even argue that such imagery would have made Apple less successful, as it might have made its messages feel more staged, more manipulative, and less authentic. What's made Apple's messaging successful is that it doesn't really *try* to be anything. It simply acts like itself—which is one of Simplicity's guiding lights. It's more believable, it's more authentic, it's more simple.

Steve's aversion to choosing "hero" people for ads began to fade with the introduction of iPhoto and iMovie. Since the value of these applications was in their ability to share heartwarming family moments, it would have been hard to do that without showing real people. Steve was as picky as you'd expect him to have been. He didn't want to cast one person who might be a turnoff to another segment of the audience we were trying to reach—and our target was "everyone." We were able to get past this discussion because we mapped out a number of ads that featured a wide range of people over the course of time. Young families, old couples, proud dads, we'd have them all.

Over the years, Apple's communications have evolved as much as its products. As the company's devices have started focusing more on our personal lives, human images have become more common. I've seen babies in Apple ads, and a puppy or two as well. All of which are fine. The Official Simplicity Handbook does not contain a clause forbidding the use of human images. The point is that human images are only one means of expressing humanity.

Even during stages in its past when Apple rarely used imagery of human beings, it was widely regarded as the most human technology company on earth. Its humanity was achieved primarily through "intelligent wit." Here we must give credit to former Chiat creative director Steve Hayden, who led the charge on the original Macintosh. Students of advertising would do well to go back and read the ads Hayden wrote in the early days of Macintosh. He gave Apple a voice that was distinct, simple, and seemingly everlasting.

Apple's marketing success has always been grounded in real-speak. That's not to say it doesn't get carried away with adjectives. It's certainly given "magical" and "revolutionary" a good workout in recent years. But overall, there's nothing tricky or manipulative about the way Apple talks to its current and potential customers.

Apple's tone is consistent with its core values—with Simplicity being core value number one. Steve Jobs created products that speak his customers' language, and he always insisted that Apple speak in that language. The result is that Apple feels "authentic" at every point of customer contact, from ad to website to purchase to the look and feel of every product. That kind of consistency goes a long way toward creating a sense of Simplicity, and it's one of the most difficult things for a marketer to do. Not coincidentally, it's one of the things Apple has down cold.

Successful brands have this kind of authenticity. For that matter, successful people have this kind of authenticity. Simplicity requires that you have a set of core values that pervade everything you do—and everything you say.

Simplicity is what makes people feel like they know you, understand you, and ultimately trust you.

Engineering Humanity

By any standard, Apple's rise from near death in 1997 to the world's most valuable company in 2011 is breathtaking. It will be studied in business schools for decades to come—most likely by students using iPads instead of textbooks.

Today Apple sits at or near the top of virtually every list that contains the words "popular brand" or "loved brand." It's the "loved" part that makes most other companies feel pangs of jealousy. Strong customer loyalty translates to repeat sales and creates evangelists who recruit friends, family, and colleagues. Loyalty like this feeds on itself, receiving a new jolt with each successive product introduction.

Put simply, Apple is very good at winning people's hearts. It understands how to get invited into people's lives, delight them with new devices, and make its relationship with customers uncomplicated. Apple's love of Simplicity is readily visible at every stage in the customer relationship: from the ads that create interest to the buying experience at the Apple Store to use of the products themselves to the support provided.

In effect, Apple has built an ecosystem of Simplicity.

In the last decade, Apple has revolutionized three product categories— music, phones, and tablets—with iPod, iPhone, and iPad. It's an extraordinary story when you stop to think that Apple's journey began with something so basic as the Apple II desktop computer. The difference between the Apple II and an iPad is akin to the difference between a Model T and an interstellar cruiser.

If Apple's quest is to push human capabilities forward and to make technology more and more human, then iPad represents its most important milestone to date. More visibly than any of Apple's previous innovations, iPad demonstrates Apple's affection for making technology a natural extension of our humanity.

That old Apple II line, "The most personal computer," would actually be a perfect descriptor for iPad. It really is a computer, many times more powerful than our earliest computers, and it's hard to imagine any device being more personal. It's easily carried. It's easily learned. It brings you closer to friends and family. And it works by simple human touch, which is a transforming experience.

It was when Steve Jobs introduced iPad that Apple started to go so heavy on the "magic" word. It showed up in Steve's presentation, the official iPad video, the Apple press release, and print and TV ads. Though some bucked at that kind of hype, it's not hard to understand why Steve thought it was such a good descriptor.

Walt Mossberg, writing for the *Wall Street Journal*, said, "I believe this beautiful new touch-screen device from Apple has the potential to change portable computing profoundly. . . . It could even help, eventually, to propel the finger-driven, multitouch user interface ahead of the mouse-driven interface that has prevailed for decades."

Mark Brown, writing for *Wired UK*, said that after twenty-eight days, "I still caress it and make evangelical speeches about how it's so easy to use and so joyous to navigate."

Indeed, just navigating the web on iPad is enough to make most people realize they've entered a different world. We've been using the mouse to control our computers so long, most have come to believe it's "natural" to cause movement on the screen by moving an offscreen mouse. But it isn't. What's really natural is to simply touch the screen to explore the item you're interested in viewing.

In this way, iPad brought with it a new dimension in Simplicity. Controlling apps by touch feels obvious, as if this is the way computers should have worked from the beginning. It makes the mouse feel like some jerry-rigged solution.

By creating such a human-centric computer, Apple not only gave developers a platform on which to build more amazing apps, it illuminated the path by which technology can move forward. Not just for itself but for the whole industry—which is busy following suit.

It's a good time to be human.

Humanity for Business or Pleasure

Of iPad's many endearing traits, there's one that didn't get quite as much press as the others: iPad has the unique ability to make friends with anyone.

It's instantly seductive to young and old, doctors and scientists, students and teachers, musicians and accountants, virtually every type of person and every type of business. It's a tribute to the power of Simplicity—and proof that its appeal has no limitations.

Back in chapter 3, we were discussing the fact that unlike other computer makers, Apple doesn't normally dilute its marketing plan by separately targeting its business and consumer audiences. Like iPhone before it, iPad concentrates on a larger demographic group: humankind.

What Apple chooses to do is simply open people's eyes to the possibilities, then leave them to self-select how they might use the device in their own lives. More than anything, the marketing message is simply that iPad will change the way you look at the world. Apple gives us glimpses of many apps, things that could be used by a range of people for business or pleasure.

While traditional marketers might complain that you'll turn off the business user if you show games, or you'll turn off the casual user if you show business functions, Apple ignores such traditional—and limiting—advice. It adds to the wonder of iPad that it can so beautifully adapt to the life of its owner, whatever kind of life that may be.

If you'd like to see Complexity at work, consider the way Research In Motion chose to introduce its iPad competitor, PlayBook. In an attempt to leverage its BlackBerry heritage as the first choice of business users—and to therefore differentiate itself from iPad—it positioned PlayBook as the tablet for the business crowd. It went so far as to introduce PlayBook on its posters and web ads with this headline:

Amateur hour is over.

However, because RIM knows that businesspeople are human beings as well, it simultaneously showed the more human uses of its tablet, featuring games, movies, and social sites. So what it communicated was that PlayBook was all business—except for all those times when it was fun and games. Not the clearest way to position a product. As of this book's publication, it wasn't a particularly effective one, either. In PlayBook's first full quarter after being launched in April 2011, RIM shipped 200,000 Play-Books (and that's "shipped," not sold), versus the 9.25 million iPads sold by Apple. In other words it took Apple less than two days to sell more devices than RIM shipped in the entire quarter.

Simplicity calls for a clear strategy, followed by consistent messaging. RIM came up with a strategy that played off its strength—a tablet for the pros—but its ads were anything but consistent. In fact, its product was anything but consistent. Oddly, though it was targeting the business crowd, the first PlayBook didn't even include an email function. It had to be "tethered" to a BlackBerry phone to access email through that device. Amateur hour, indeed.

Meanwhile, Apple continues to follow its simpler route, advertising to consumers and businesses alike. And guess what? It continues to sell by the millions, and there has yet to be a backlash of angry consumers or businesspeople complaining that they haven't been spoken to exclusively.

Simplicity has universal appeal.

Born to Be Human

The laws of Simplicity are in effect across every department at Apple. But nowhere is that more evident than within the secret chambers where Apple products are born—the design labs.

Being a key part of Simplicity, human-centricity is baked into every new Apple product from the time it's just a twinkle in the designer's eye.

The exact process by which Apple devices are conceived and created remains secret, but Steve Jobs revealed in interviews that he and his executive team would meet regularly to review the newest ideas. The team would determine what ideas were worthy of further development and which should be passed over.

This would be the moment when a new idea gets measured against the principles of Simplicity, and its ability to connect on a human level would be gauged.

Of course, no Apple designer would dare present an idea that wasn't Simplicity compliant, but some ideas would succeed more than others. Following the discussion, the council of elders would rule.

For the sake of posterity, I wish Apple would record some of these meetings so that the goings-on might be revealed sometime in the future. It would be fascinating to listen to the conversations that took place over the initial concept of iPhone, for example. But fear not. Merely by looking at the history of Apple products in this decade, it doesn't take a genius to understand what Apple demands of its products.

Simplicity is an open book.

The concept has to be quick. The customer has to get it in a second—like "phone, Internet, and iPod, all in one." Customers need to be able to pick it up and start using it instantly. Most important, it has to improve our lives by an order of magnitude over what's already available or create an entirely new category by itself.

That last qualification is one that Steve Jobs used to talk about all the way back at NeXT. He made it a point to say that in the technology business, the only truly meaningful change is a 10x improvement over what came before. A product needs to have this level of importance attached to it if it is to get noticed and gain traction. Some of those measurements are subjective, of course, but when you look back at Apple's big hits, they follow the pattern. For a live demonstration, hold the original iPhone up next to the BlackBerry that was popular when iPhone was first launched. Leaps of magnitude are hard to ignore.

If a new idea at Apple fails in any of the important measures, you can be sure it will be hit with the Simple Stick. That will either improve it or put it out of its misery.

The Battle Between Numbers and Humans

The digital revolution has spawned an unfathomably large volume of statistics. No client or agency is complete unless it's equipped with experts to analyze the numbers generated by the trail of clicks we leave behind as we explore the Internet.

A company like Dell is consumed by these numbers. There are goals attached to every project, and if the clicks don't match the goals, somebody's in trouble. It's not hard to appreciate why Dell's managers place so much emphasis on performance metrics. Quite a few get bonuses based on these hard numbers.

For companies that operate in this manner, it's just smart business. With all this data available, it would be foolish to operate any other way. Numbers are your friend. Just look what the Oakland A's did in *Moneyball*. Using the information gleaned from raw statistics, they were able to build a winning baseball team without a Yankees-sized budget.

However, the reality isn't quite as romantic. To appreciate this, you need only look at Dell's place in the world versus Apple's. In Dell you see a company that places the highest priority on analytics but struggles mightily when it comes to winning customers' hearts. In Apple you see a company that puts its priorities on delighting its customers, which it does consistently—and generates far higher profits than Dell as a result.

Steve Jobs was one of the most forward-thinking people on this planet, yet he was refreshingly old-fashioned when it came to the use of analytics. He demanded all the information he could get, and he would digest every bit of it—but he took it all in context.

He never lost sight of the fact that at the end of the day, technology is about people: what stirs their imaginations, what keeps them satisfied, and what makes them smile. He would never sacrifice that kind of connection in favor of a decision that somehow got Apple a few more clicks on its website.

Steve saw the slavish devotion to numbers as a big-company behavior. He would never have his head stuck in the numbers, no matter how big Apple got. He would eagerly consume the data that would pour in, but in the end he made his decisions based on head and heart—like every good human should. It keeps things simple.

There's a theme that Steve played back many times in his public presentations. He said that Apple stands at the intersection of technology and liberal arts—and this was the essence of Steve. That was the spirit in which he judged product design and it was the spirit in which he made marketing decisions. He would never put his blind faith in statistics or judge the worth of an idea by the number he saw at the bottom of a spreadsheet. Ideas were everything to Steve and he knew that great ideas didn't usually show up in traditional ways.

Steve recognized the difference between a fact and an emotion. He understood that the intangible and the unprovable can be the most important parts of building a brand. The idea of running his business through analytics alone sat no better with Steve than the idea of asking people on the street what kind of product they'd like Apple to build.

On several occasions, Steve used a famous quote from Henry Ford: "If

I asked people what they wanted, they'd say a faster horse." In his mind, it was Apple's job to dream up the things that people *can't* imagine. He knew that once they lived with a great product, they wouldn't be able to imagine living without it. In a 1998 *BusinessWeek* interview, Steve said:

> *It's really hard to design products by focus groups. A lot of times, people don't know what they want until you show it to them.*

As uninterested as Apple is in using focus groups to inspire new products, it's even less interested in using focus groups to develop its marketing messages. Out of respect for Simplicity, Steve trusted his small group of smart people to do the best job. He didn't consider validation from outsiders to be very valid.

I can sense the squirming on this one. "That's crazy." "How can you invest millions of dollars without some indication of success?" "It's just irresponsible."

Well, again, if anyone requires proof that Apple's methods result in better work, it's been on public display since Steve returned to Apple in 1997. Apple's marketing consistently outshines that of every other company in its category, and probably 95 percent of those in other categories as well. Apple's ads are well thought out, humorously appealing to a mass audience, perfectly focused, and 100 percent focus group free.

Like all companies, Apple is perfectly capable of filling a room with smart marketing people. Like few companies, Apple is willing to let the final decision remain in that room. Given the results it's achieved by following this path for the last fifteen years, its customers would have it no other way.

Apple isn't interested in ideas that try to please everyone. Those are the ideas that end up stripped of their character, feeling calculated and worst of all—less human.

Chapter 9
Think Skeptic

During my earliest days working on Apple's advertising, back when John Sculley was CEO, one of the agency's writers created a sign to hang over his office door. It read:

When® lawyers™ roamed* the† earth.℠

I would have thought it was funnier if I hadn't myself fallen victim to the legal forces that often swirl around clients and agencies. After just a year or two in the business, I found myself testifying in court over an ad I had written for Chiat on behalf of a New York–based airline. I was innocent, I swear.

Lawyers play a big role in the marketing business. They come in handy when a company gets sued for a few billion dollars. They're also on hand to make sure that the wacky guys in the creative department don't do something everyone will live to regret. In fact, the creative guys often get it from two sides, because there is normally a team of lawyers inside both the agency and the client. Every ad that gets produced has to be cleared by both sets of lawyers, each of which is out to protect its own interests.

Even though I was familiar with the process, I was still surprised one day to get an email from the Apple lawyers concerning a newspaper ad that was going to run in just three days. The agency's lawyers had already approved it. Steve Jobs had already approved it. Now, at the eleventh hour, Apple's lawyers were saying that they had some problems with it.

The ad in question, coming before Apple made the transition to Intel processors, made the claim that the new Power Macintosh computers actually outperformed the fastest Intel-powered PCs, and offered some benchmark testing to prove it. The lawyers took issue with four points in the copy, fearing that we might face a legal challenge from Intel.

Doing my duty, I sent a note to Steve advising him that there was a wrench in the works—his own legal team. I succinctly described the four problem areas and asked for guidance.

Fortunately, Steve wasn't going to allow Complexity to do its dirty work. Just minutes after I hit the "send" button, his reply landed in my inbox. It wasn't the most verbose email I'd ever received. But the first sentence so eloquently put things into perspective:

Fuck the lawyers.

Take Advice, Not Orders

Let us pause for a moment to savor those words. I've certainly found them inspirational over the years.

They actually do an excellent job of capturing Steve's built-in skepticism—a trait that served Simplicity well. If he were to hear an opinion that was contrary to his own, or inconsistent with his vision, his instinct was to doubt its validity. After all, how could it be that the world wouldn't work as he wanted it to?

But I'm going to call this a "healthy skepticism." Because the fact is, many of the expert opinions we hear in business are unnecessarily limiting. They may be spoken by someone who hasn't given the situation enough thought, or doesn't understand all the nuances, or is just being far more cautious than you wish to be—as Steve believed his lawyers were being in this case.

I'm sure many of us have experienced the frustration of working with a leader who isn't nearly skeptical enough—someone who blindly accepts the opinion of his or her legal department, for example, and treats it more as a court order than counsel.

This is not to say that Steve's skepticism led him to ignore his experts' advice. It just means that he would consider their advice in context of other evidence, his larger goals for the company, and Common Sense.

As Apple became more successful and competition intensified, Steve likely considered his lawyers as essential as his engineers. He relied on their expertise and judgment to help Apple protect its intellectual property and trademarks around the world.

But as we all know, Steve was also committed to his vision and believed in his own judgment. While he would have had great respect for a lawyer's opinion, he didn't expect a lawyer to be skilled in the nuances of marketing, or be aware of other considerations that might surround a specific decision. So he had no qualms vetoing conservative advice when he believed that a degree of risk was warranted—as he did in the case above. Personally I enjoyed the fact that he did it with such swiftness and style.

A true friend of Simplicity will at least remain open to the possibility of rejecting an expert's advice after considering other factors, as opposed to reflexively implementing it.

In case you were wondering what consequences resulted from Steve's decision to spurn his lawyers' advice and run that anti-Intel ad unchanged, there were none. The ad ran in its original form, Apple made its point, Intel got a bit steamed, and nobody went to jail. Steve was right again.

iPhone Versus iPhone

It was going to be one of the most important Apple events in history. Steve was looking forward to getting onstage and saying "This is iPhone."

The product was ready. The ads were ready. It was all perfect—except for the annoying little fact that Cisco was already selling a device with the same name. Of course we don't hear much about the Cisco iPhone these days. But that's only because Steve exercised his skepticism when he learned that Cisco's trademark would stand in the way of his plan.

The Cisco iPhone was aptly named. It was an Internet phone that connected to the wireless network in your home, allowing you to make calls on Skype and similar services. It could also do a number of other tricks, such as access your music and photos.

Steve, as you might imagine, was not happy that Cisco was using the iPhone name for its largely invisible device when he thought it was such a perfect name for his world-changing device. Never mind that Cisco was doing what so many companies were doing in the naming department— borrowing Apple's "i" to cash in on the i-wave. Clearly there was some debate going on in Steve's office about what to do, because for those working on the marketing side, as launch day approached, one day it would be "iPhone" and the next day it would be "quick, we need some alternatives." By most indications, going ahead with the iPhone announcement would open Apple up to a serious lawsuit.

According to published statements from Cisco sources, an agreement with Apple was reached and papers delivered to Apple for signature the day before Steve was set to introduce iPhone. But Apple never signed the papers. The next morning Steve got up and started the iPhone revolution by unveiling the device—and without ever settling the issue with Cisco.

As Cisco told the story, it was shocked at this turn of events and had every intention of suing. However, another version of events also got some airplay. In this version, Cisco had registered the iPhone trademark in 1999, but its trademark had lapsed in 2005 for lack of use—before it actually started shipping its iPhone. Possibly it was because the situation was somewhat murky that, even though Steve had reached an agreement with Cisco, he decided at the last minute not to sign. He would shoot first and ask questions later.

Cisco did in fact begin a legal action immediately following the launch of iPhone, but then quickly reached an agreement with Apple on "undisclosed terms." Reportedly, Apple agreed to do some comarketing with Cisco, though no one on earth seems to be aware of any such thing ever happening. If he actually took part in it, this negotiation would have been an interesting Steve Jobs performance to watch.

The greater point, though, is that Steve saw extremely high value in the name "iPhone" and was undeterred by the potentially tough legal road ahead. He was looking at what he'd gain by launching the device with that name and the long-term benefit of having an iPhone subbrand. He was determined to push hard in a situation where most would have gone the safe route and simply chosen another name.

The ending of this adventure is well known. The value of the iPhone name is now incalculable, reducing the cost of this legal adventure to utter insignificance. As a subbrand, iPhone is now nearly as strong as the Apple brand itself—for all the reasons that Steve preferred it. It's simple, obvious, and easy to remember. And it's all because Steve believed that the name was attainable even when the indications were negative.

Now just think for a minute about your own company, or the companies you've worked with. If caught in a similar situation, about to launch a widely anticipated product, unable to positively secure the name, and facing a significant legal risk—what would the decision be? Exactly.

This was a case of Steve wanting what he wanted. Could Chiat or his own people have come up with another name that would be risk-free? Absolutely. And they came up with quite a few. But in Steve's mind the name iPhone was too perfect to give up on, and it was practically by sheer will that Apple came to own it.

While Apple was playing for very high stakes, the same principles apply to our more everyday decisions. It's about evaluating advice in context and having the strength to move ahead when the rewards outweigh the risks.

In Appreciation of Skeptical Lawyers

Creative people in advertising don't normally have a love of lawyers. Too many great ideas have been killed (or seriously injured) by legal minds, and the pain often lingers. Still, that doesn't mean we can't be deeply thankful when a lawyer's skepticism helps derail a bad idea that's picking up steam.

At one of our regular agency meetings, about a year after the launch of iMac, Steve walked into the room giddy with enthusiasm for a new idea. If it was someone else's idea, he didn't make that distinction. On this day he was pitching an idea to the rest of the room rather than the other way around.

According to Apple's calculations, the one millionth iMac was about to be sold. That was huge news. Remember, Apple had undergone some very tough times, and iMac was the first new computer to be launched by Steve upon his return to the company. To have sold a million iMacs in a relatively short time was proof that something very right was happening, and it deserved some serious fanfare.

Steve's idea was to do a Willy Wonka routine with it. Just as Wonka did in the movie, Steve wanted to put a golden certificate representing the millionth iMac inside the box of one iMac, and publicize that fact. Whoever opened the lucky iMac box would be refunded the purchase price and be flown to Cupertino, where he or she (and, presumably, the accompanying family) would be taken on a tour of the Apple campus.

Steve had already instructed his internal creative group to design a prototype golden certificate, which he shared with us. But the killer was that Steve wanted to go all out on this. He wanted to meet the lucky winner in full Willy Wonka garb. Yes, complete with top hat and tails.

It was one of those ideas that made everyone in the room laugh, but the funniest part was that Steve seemed so enamored of it. He saw the potential to get massive PR for iMac and Apple, and he was more than willing to do his share by donning the costume. Unlike what happened in the movie, however, the winner would not become the new owner of Apple. He or she wouldn't even get a junior assistant CEO position. It would all be for fun—along with the big, juicy headlines.

We left that meeting with instructions to look into the logistics and legality of the idea. Fortunately, the legal issues were restrictive. For one, California regulations required that this be classified as a sweepstakes, which meant that there had to be a "no purchase required" provision. It would be impossible to make that golden certificate work under these rules, so it would have to be more of a drawing. Which meant anyone off the street could win, and the odds were that whoever did win probably wouldn't even have purchased an iMac. Faced with the restrictions imposed by lawyers, Steve decided it wasn't worth it.

We all breathed a sigh of relief—and the world was denied the opportunity to see Steve in his Willy Wonka suit.

Under the Yoke of Lawyers

One of the more dubious ad campaigns I've ever participated in turned out to be one of the best examples of legal opinions gone unquestioned.

At the midpoint of my stay at Intel's agency, Intel requested that we come up with an umbrella campaign that would support all of its processor lines. At this time, the relationship between agency and client was showing signs of strain. So, with the stakes getting higher, and the agency running out of wiggle room, our president decided to take no chances. He expanded our small group of smart people by inviting one of his favorite creative people to join the brainstorming process, and he invited the CEO to join him in the approval process. We would do everything necessary to "get this one right."

After a week of feverish work, the entire project group—creative people, account people, and agency management—met around a table in the president's office.

After we reviewed several campaign ideas, our special guest creative person rose to make his pitch. His Scottish accent was endearing and somehow enhanced his reputation as a quirky guy. He was not wearing a kilt, as he was sometimes known to do. He launched into his presentation.

It played out like a Hollywood vision of what a creative presentation should be—even though such visions are rarely accurate. Our Scottish friend told a story about Intel that described its positive attitude, its ability to overcome obstacles and grant even the most difficult wishes of its customers. His story built toward a logical conclusion: Intel was all about empowerment; it did exactly what it set out to do, even against the most formidable odds. Therefore, its spirit could be described by a single word. It was one of the most common words in the English language, yet it was a word that would have the power to reshape the Intel brand. This all-powerful, supercompelling word was . . .

Yes.

The other creative people in the room reacted the way you probably just did. To us, it was as if someone had let the air out of the balloon. But our president and CEO ate it up. They loved the idea of owning the word "yes," and they loved the graphic that went with it. That magic word sat upon a large, blue, round wafer of silicon (the raw product in the chip manufacturing process) and would be shown full frame at the end of each commercial.

The idea was developed, approved, and turned into a series of TV spots. Unfortunately, early in the campaign's life a legal problem surfaced in Germany. Some obscure company was claiming ownership of the "yes" idea. (Funny, because for the sake of our standing in the creative community, many of us were doing our best *not* to claim ownership.) This, of course, is one of the problems that comes with being a large multinational company. Like Apple, Intel was a lightning rod for lawsuits. Those who sue in cases like this often operate on the hope that the company might prefer to make the case go away by opening its wallet.

Intel didn't disappoint. The German company had its payday and Intel went on its merry way. The campaign continued to run in Germany and everywhere else. However, one thing had changed: Now Intel's legal department was spooked. It was summer at this point, and we received word that Intel's attorneys were killing the campaign. It would not be allowed to run past the end of the year.

It was explained that even though they still believed the German lawsuit was without merit, the lawyers were now of the belief that if one company had figured out a way to sue, others might do the same. This despite the fact that the same lawyers had originally done their due diligence and declared the campaign to be legally safe and not susceptible to anyone else's copyright claims.

This was a surprising decision to both the agency and Intel's marketing group. Intel had faced a legal challenge, made it go away at relatively low cost, won permission to continue with the campaign it had invested in—and now it was too nervous to take any more chances.

Unlike Steve Jobs, who vetoed his lawyers' advice so that he might run the advertising he believed in and took the name iPhone when its ownership was in question, Intel considered its lawyers' decision to be more of a ruling than a request.

For Simplicity to gain the upper hand, there must be someone in the room willing to stick his neck out for it. In this case, everyone in the food chain was willing to go through the months of new creative development and testing that would be required before a replacement campaign could be chosen. No one seemed to be concerned about the damage that might be inflicted upon the brand by switching campaigns twice in the same year. To the public, Intel would not appear to be a fan of Simplicity.

Complexity gets double credit here. The campaign was born of a team that exceeded the small-group-of-smart-people limit, with too many approvers, in a climate of political pressure. And it was derailed by corporate attorneys who might not have seen the bigger marketing picture. Therefore, in a rare feat, Complexity not only gave birth to this campaign but was also responsible for its death.

The happy ending to this story is that Intel never came to legally own the word "yes." You are free to use it in conversation without paying royalties.

Death Threats Work Wonders

Enough about "yes." Let's move on to the word "no."

When someone comes up with an idea in business, this is a word that is heard way too often. There are always a thousand reasons why something can't be done—only a few of which can't be circumvented with creative thinking. So when a colleague or vendor says no, you need to take that with a large grain of salt. More often than not, what they really mean to say is that it would take too much effort, it's not the way we ordinarily do things, it would be too costly, or any number of other excuses.

Sometimes the impossible is truly impossible. Other times it is merely improbable. So it pays to take a long, hard look at negative responses before you throw in the towel. Some of us have the unique ability to make instant judgments about what's possible. Steve Jobs was one.

Rarely would Steve tolerate a negative response when he wanted something done. Unless you could prove beyond a shadow of a doubt that there was an immovable object in the way, he expected you to do the job. If you couldn't, he'd find someone who could—and that wouldn't bode well for your future as part of the group.

When I was out with colleagues, we would sometimes lapse into impromptu psychoanalysis that might explain how Steve acquired his chronic unwillingness to take no for an answer. One explanation is obvious. Steve started Apple in 1976, when he was only twenty-one years old. Prior to that, he had only worked short stints at HP and Atari. So unlike most people in this world, Steve had spent little of his working years reporting to a supervisor. For virtually all of his adult life, he was the one who gave the orders. He expected things to get done.

This demanding behavior was ever present in Steve, no matter whom he was dealing with. It wasn't about being a bully, it was simply Steve's way of never settling for anything less than he imagined. You only needed to run afoul of Steve's expectations once to understand what was expected of you and to make sure it never happened again. I was fortunate because I learned my lesson early and got it out of the way.

Back in the early days of iMac, we planned to introduce some new models by running a sixteen-page insert in *Time* magazine. After several weeks of development, photography, and writing, the insert was nearing completion. Steve told us he wanted to see it in *Time* two weeks from that date. When I told this to the agency's print producer, she had a good laugh. We could rush the actual printing of the inserts, but then we'd be at the mercy of *Time*. The newsweeklies have firm production timetables, and inserts require weeks of preparation to accommodate the mechanics of taking delivery on millions of inserts and incorporating them into the press run. With my new understanding, I got back to Steve with the information. I told him there was no way *Time* could accommodate us. It would be several weeks at best.

"That's bullshit," said Steve. He'd hear nothing of it. He noted that *Time* put out a magazine with about sixty pages every week and did it with only a few days of prep.

I gave him all the reasons why it was different with inserts. However, as I was defending our position, I could feel my argument getting flimsier. That's when Steve lobbed his little bomb.

"If you guys can't do it, I'll bet Arnold can figure out how to do it pretty quick."

Arnold, you will recall, was the other agency Steve had considered back when he had just returned to Apple and was contemplating a new agency. Arnold had been eager to get the business before, and it would be even more eager to get its foot in the door now. The last thing we needed was to have Arnold march in and do the job we had said couldn't be done. This is how agencies lose accounts.

So within minutes, I was back with the agency producer, telling her that the situation had just gone from urgent to critical. We had to figure out a way to get the insert in *Time* quickly or we'd be opening a door that we didn't want to open. She went off to make her calls, and I crossed my fingers.

A well-crafted combination of begging, threatening, and crying was enough to get *Time* to give us a break. Get us the materials quickly and we'll make it happen in two weeks, they said.

Great news, but now I had a little mess to clean up. I'd just put my credibility on the line by telling Steve what I had previously been told myself—that there was no way to circumvent *Time*'s rules. Steve didn't believe me, I'd stuck to my story, and now I was going to have to tell him he was right after all. We'd found a way to make it work.

True, I was basing my case on expert testimony, but I'd made the mistake of not relying on my own Common Sense as Steve had done. I'd succeeded in reinforcing his belief that he should never take no for an answer. Unfortunately, I also gave him good reason to think twice about taking the agency's word about what was possible and what wasn't.

We tend to remember our moments of trauma, so this story has stuck with me over the years. It's made me wary whenever I hear the word "no." For the sake of Simplicity, it's a good idea to probe thoroughly when you run into a negative response. It might just be that you're asking someone to go above and beyond what's normal—but that's how you get above-normal results. If there are rules, chances are they can be broken. If you let someone off the hook, it's your idea that will be diminished in the end.

Years later, I spent some time with one of Dell's chief designers, and he had a similar story to share. So I don't blow his cover, I'll call him Mick.

Mick's story surrounded the birth of Dell's would-be competitor to the superthin MacBook Air, the ill-fated Dell Adamo. Though this laptop was destined to land with a thud, struggle to get noticed, and ultimately be put to sleep two years later, there was excitement in the air back at the beginning. Creating a computer like this was a first for Dell.

I had just come from the agency's first Adamo briefing. While awaiting my taxi back to the hotel, I bumped into Mick and we sat down for a private chat in the Dell lobby. During that conversation, we got to talking about delivering on impossible schedules, which triggered my memory of the *Time* insert for Apple. I told Mick the story of how I had been bruised by failing to question what was really possible.

"Exactly what happened to me with Adamo," said Mick. He went on to tell me about the meetings that spawned Dell's ultrathin computer.

Many months before, Mick had met with Ron Garriques, then head of Dell's Consumer division. Like many in the computer business, Ron was eager to build a computer that was truly buzz-worthy. He'd decided that Dell should get cracking on an ultrathin laptop because, now that Apple had launched the MacBook Air, thin was clearly the new cool thing in the industry. (Far be it from Dell to be the first in a category.)

Garriques asked Mick to return with a timetable for this project, so off went Mick to consult with his engineers. Those who would actually have to design and build a laptop this thin thought it would take about a year to get it to market. Creating an ultrathin laptop is far more difficult than designing a desktop PC. It requires serious miniaturization, and this degree of engineering takes time.

Mick shared this information with Garriques—who did not take the news well at all. Though Garriques had little in common with Steve Jobs, he had mastered one principle of Simplicity. He wanted what he wanted, and he wasn't about to take no for an answer. And what he wanted now was an ultrathin laptop in half the time it would normally take. Having pushed his engineers as far as he could, Mick could only stand his ground. He was told unequivocally that the timetable could not be shortened.

Frustrated by this news, Garriques reached into his bag of tricks. In his previous life, he had been with Motorola's phone group, where miniaturization was a way of life. If Motorola's engineers could pack all that amazing technology into something that fits in your pocket, he figured that they should be able to work miracles for a laptop. So he went outside Dell to pull in some of the engineers with whom he had worked at Motorola. They promised a laptop in six months.

Once Garriques had what he wanted, Mick found himself in a position with which I was intimately familiar. Mick became the guy who had said it couldn't be done, when in reality it could.

Now, if Garriques could rise to the Simplicity challenge, refuse to take no for an answer, and get his spiffy new laptop in the time frame he wanted, why then did Adamo turn into the failure it was?

Back at the beginning of this book, I mentioned that Simplicity was an all-or-none proposition, that you can't just choose the pieces à la carte. Garriques was not a disciple of Simplicity; he was just an executive who wanted what he wanted. Though he slammed the door on Complexity when he set the project in motion, he apparently left the key in it. The Adamo project quickly drowned in a sea of Complexity, from its pricing and availability to its marketing and reliability issues.

Adamo was a $2,500 laptop from a company known for $600 laptops. It was a product you had to hold to appreciate, yet it could only be ordered online. It was advertised with ads that belonged in *Vogue*, featuring ultra-high-fashion models, but actually ran in the business press, online and offline. Months after its launch, Adamo was selling in the thousands while MacBook Air was selling in the millions. Even with a redesign a year later, Adamo could never recover, and finally Dell just gave up on it altogether.

But they sure did design it fast.

Standing Up for Details

People often talk about the "unboxing experience" that comes with buying an Apple product. YouTube has countless videos documenting, step by step and piece by piece, the opening of an Apple product box. To the outsider, this is simply another example of Apple fanboyism. It's just a box, right?

To Apple, a box is hardly "just a box." The company takes incredible care to ensure that the entire customer experience is consistently first quality—and that first moment, when the customer is going through the packaging, is a significant part of that experience.

To say that Apple takes its packaging seriously is an understatement. The group responsible for package design at Apple works in a locked-down room inside the larger creative group headquarters. What they do in there is every bit as secret as what the engineers do in their inner sanctum. Makes sense, considering that the packaging reveals more about the product specs than any glimpse of the product itself.

Actually, Apple has some dark times in its packaging past. Some people will remember that during Steve's exile, the company instituted some major cost-cutting initiatives. Gone were the glossy white boxes with color printing, and in their place came plain brown cardboard boxes featuring just one or two colors. I have one of these things in my attic, and I can't bear to toss it because it's such a vivid reminder of how Apple's sensibilities have changed. It's an old PowerBook box, and inside there are just a few molded egg carton–type pieces of cardboard designed to hold various parts of the product. It's one of the least elegant, most humdrum bits of packaging you can imagine.

As Apple's values and priorities evolved—thanks to the return of Steve Jobs—these kinds of details would become hugely important once again. So much so that otherwise rational and intelligent people would be driven to make unboxing videos.

The people who design Apple's packaging are incredibly talented. But, obviously, they don't physically manufacture the packaging in their secret room. They have to rely on various vendors to help them realize their dreams. They also have to deal with people who say, "Sorry, can't be done."

A few years ago, a senior package designer at Apple related a story about the depth of care that goes into Apple package design.

The reason Apple goes to extremes, of course, is that it wants customers to get that feeling of quality from the moment they touch the box. The specific details may not register, but people will get that feeling of "cool" that makes them all the more eager to get to the goody inside. In this way the packaging works rather like the Apple Store. People may not pick out specific details, but they sense the thoughtful and elegant design of the store. Every detail matters, whether it's noticed or not.

With great pride, the package designer told me how Apple had refused to take no for an answer when a vendor reported back that a certain package feature was problematic and needed to be changed.

The designer had created a gorgeous box worthy of a new Apple device. Inside, the product sat in a recessed compartment supported by a tiny piece of Styrofoam. That piece was so delicate, it was causing a problem in the manufacturing process. It was melting from the heat of the molding machines. The vendor duly told Apple that it wasn't a solvable problem—the box had to be redesigned to accommodate the laws of physics.

The package design team wasn't pleased. They had a vision, and now outside forces were interfering with that vision. Plus, Steve Jobs had already approved this design, as he had approved every detail of the product itself. Someone would either have to tell Steve the package design needed to be altered or push back with the vendor.

True to the Apple way, the designers did not want to compromise. In a not-so-veiled threat, they told the vendor that Apple wasn't going to redesign the package—instead he would have to redesign his machines. If the metal molds were getting too hot, why not make new molds from aluminum?

At great expense, that's what the vendor did. Soon the Styrofoam pieces were being churned out without a hitch. Owners of these particular Apple devices were able to enjoy the ideal unboxing experience—even though it's doubtful that even one of them ever noticed that little piece of Styrofoam hidden within.

The Apple designers recognized that when the vendor said, "It can't be done," what he really meant was that it couldn't be done without extraordinary effort. It's amazing what people can accomplish when they see a juicy account about to walk out the door.

Ignoring the Naysayers: Inventing the Apple Store

Steve Jobs's speech at Stanford struck a chord with many because he was so clearly speaking from the heart. He talked about the importance of discovering a path that will lead to true fulfillment in life. It was a particularly daunting task for him, because he was speaking to a group who had just finished college, and he had dropped out almost before he started.

But his words to these businesspeople-to-be were of equal value to those who have been in business for decades:

> *Don't let the noise of other's opinions drown out your own inner voice.*
> *And most important, have the courage to follow your heart and intuition.*

Steve wasn't just offering advice about choosing a career path. He was describing an important rule of doing business. It's a rule that he'd always followed himself and one that had helped him ward off the evil spirit of Complexity for virtually his entire life. Sometimes it just requires a special strength to fight your way toward a goal when the naysayers are convinced you're heading down a path of doom.

Exhibit A: the Apple Stores.

In the days when Apple was showing progress in recovering from its near-death experience, it still had some extremely difficult mountains to climb. Steve was convinced that when customers actually sat down with a Mac and had someone show them how easy it was to use, they were easy to convince. The problem was finding a way to have that conversation. There were very few stores where you could just walk in and get familiar with a Mac, and even fewer stores where the salespeople cared enough to demonstrate it properly. Apple had just started its online Apple Store, and that was a convenience—but it wasn't a personal experience. It didn't allow Apple to have those one-on-one conversations.

So in 1997 Steve announced a deal with CompUSA, in which that national retail chain would create an Apple "store within a store." This partnership was greeted with some enthusiasm, since customers would instantly gain the ability to touch Apple products in-store, nationally, at convenient locations.

It didn't exactly work as planned. People did have a place to go, but Apple's presence in CompUSA was usually way back in a corner. You had to go looking for it and walk through a maze of PC equipment to get there. If you asked a CompUSA salesman how that iMac compared to a PC, he'd be more than happy to show you a spiffy new HP computer at a fraction of the price. He had little incentive to sell the iMac.

No, CompUSA wasn't going to solve Apple's problems. In a world of PCs, all powered by Windows, Apple was the odd duck. Convincing a customer that Apple had a superior platform required more than some dedicated space in the back of CompUSA and a halfhearted salesperson. If Apple was going to start reclaiming the market share it had lost during its dark years, it needed to do some serious "thinking different."

And so the idea of the Apple Store was born. Steve recruited Ron Johnson, famous for turning Target into a cool place to shop, to head Apple's new retail group and develop the Apple Store concept.

Today, you'd have to look far and wide to find a single person who doesn't see the value of the Apple Stores. They're widely regarded as one of the greatest retail successes in history. They've become the gold standard in the retail world, making more money per square foot than Tiffany. But clear as this may be now, it was just theory back then.

There were already vultures circling the retail skies. At that moment, they were preparing to feast on the chain of Gateway Country stores that had opened in 1996. But it wasn't hard to imagine them shifting their gaze toward Apple's new retail stores when they got hungry again. For Apple to walk down that path so starry-eyed when another computer chain was so visibly failing took some nerve.

Apple had zero experience in the retail world and only about 3 percent of the computer market (a similar market share to Gateway's). So it wasn't totally unexpected when someone like David Goldstein, president of Channel Marketing, offered his observation in a *BusinessWeek* interview:

> *I give them two years before they're turning out the lights on a very painful and expensive mistake.*

Mr. Goldstein's widely reported opinion made him the poster boy for horrifically inaccurate prognosticating.

Bloomberg Businessweek didn't do much better when it published an article with the headline "Sorry, Steve: Here's Why Apple Stores Won't Work."

Apple now has over 350 stores in the most prime real estate around the world. Mind-bogglingly, the annual total number of customers entering Apple Stores globally is actually greater than the annual combined attendance of Walt Disney Company's four biggest theme parks. As of 2012, the Apple Stores were responsible for over $14 billion of annual revenue (and nearly $5 billion in profit). The icing on the cake is that more than half of the stores' visitors are new to the Mac—so Apple's retail presence has become its most potent weapon in regaining market share. Just a few years ago, the thought that Apple could make a significant comeback against PCs was laughable—now it's just a fact of life. In mid-2012, the growth of Mac shipments outpaced that of PC shipments for the twenty-fifth consecutive quarter.

Apple was confident that if it built its shrines to Simplicity in high-traffic locations, it could begin creating the one-on-one relationships that had been lacking. Its goal was to provide a shopping experience that would be as high quality as its products.

Even if you were convinced that building the Apple Stores was the right thing for Apple to do, it was still surprising and risky to build these stores in the way it did. Rather than following Gateway with stores that had a distinctly Sears-like feel to them, Apple went the first-class route.

It hired brilliant architects and designers. It used only the highest-quality materials to bring its vision to life, even if that meant transporting materials from distant countries. And it was consistent. As dozens of new Apple Stores began to appear, each was built to the same high standards, with key flagship stores bordering on the spectacular. The Apple Store on Fifth Avenue in New York, for example, would become a famous landmark in a city of high-rises, even though it rises only thirty-two feet in the air.

In that store, the floor tiles were of a quality that could be found in only one place on earth, a quarry in Italy. The stainless steel of the support columns was born of a process that could only be found in Tokyo. The glass components were the creation of a design firm in Germany.

Apple's critics were likely rolling their eyes that the company would invest so heavily in a plan that carried such obvious risks. What they didn't realize was that Apple was building a physical representation of its brand. The Apple brand stood for quality, design, and Simplicity, and the Apple Stores brought all three of these things to life. The stores were uncluttered and inviting, with every detail fussed over.

If there is one focus at Apple that transcends all others, it's the customer experience. The goal is to give the customer a consistently great experience throughout their entire relationship with Apple. From TV ad and website to shopping to unboxing to everyday use to repair and support, Apple aims to consistently deliver the same values and speak in the same tone.

Before the Apple Stores came along, only one part of that sequence was missing: the shopping experience. Not only was it missing, it was completely out of Apple's control. It put the company in the uncomfortable position of having to depend on the quality of someone else's effort to make up for its own deficiency. Support wasn't ideal either, as customers could only communicate with Apple via phone or through independently owned service providers.

If Apple wanted to give customers a better shopping and ownership experience, it would have to take matters into its own hands. The Apple Stores would provide what was missing. Apple was skeptical of those who were skeptical of its chances, and no force on earth would keep the company from believing in its retail plans.

It's a rare idea in business that doesn't run into some form of opposition, be it internal or external to the organization. Steve Jobs learned early that if you have a great idea, you need to ignore the negativity and concentrate on moving forward.

You must also go to extremes to ensure that those great ideas survive.

Chapter 10
Think War

"You know, we could really get sued over this," said Steve. "And that might not be a bad thing."

It was 1998. Laid out in front of Steve on the boardroom table was a new ad campaign that was calculated to do more than raise eyebrows. Across two full pages of a newspaper was the giant image of a snail—carrying on its back what was then the fastest Intel chip powering PCs. If that wasn't insulting enough, this ad was the follow-up to a TV commercial that was getting heavy airplay on the major networks. Most of the ad's thirty seconds featured a close-up of the same snail, burdened by the same Intel chip, oozing its way across the screen.

Both ads made the brazen claim that the chip inside the new Macs was literally twice as fast as the Intel chip.

Steve was right. Intel would not take too kindly to this—and that was exactly the plan. Simplicity being in a constant war with Complexity, there are times when it must act with appropriate belligerence.

Bear in mind that all of this happened just months after Steve had returned to Apple, and long before Apple decided to switch its entire line of computers to Intel chips. The *Think different* ads were appearing everywhere, but iMac was still being hatched down on the engineering deck.

In those days PCs owned 97 percent of the global computer market. Almost all PCs ran on Intel processors, while Macs were built on the PowerPC chip, which had been jointly created by IBM and Motorola. Between Apple's public decline and the fact that the previous PowerPC chips weren't all that speedy, the public perception was that PCs could run circles around Macs. However, we'd just been handed a powerful weapon in the latest reports from Apple engineering. We had the benchmarks to prove that the new chip in the Power Mac G3 really did have the speed advantage over Intel's chip.

We knew full well that Intel would have a range of options if it chose to respond, with a lawsuit being option number one. "Can you imagine the story in *BusinessWeek*?" Steve said. He envisioned how the article might look in that magazine, with a big picture of the Intel chip-on-a-snail front and center in the middle of a feature story about Intel taking Apple to court. He loved it. He also knew that Intel would have to be very careful about bullying poor little Apple, which was hanging on for dear life. And it would have to think long and hard before actually taking any kind of legal action, since it would just give Apple even more publicity.

Snail was just the opening salvo in the unilaterally declared war against Intel. The creative team behind that ad, art director Michael Rylander and writer Tom Witt, dreamed up two more attacks. Soon came *Burning Bunny*, in which we literally scorched one of Intel's "bunny men"—the colorful clean-suited characters Intel had used in its own ads. In this ad, Apple apologized to Intel for "toasting it in public" with such superior benchmarks. Completing the trilogy was *Steamroller*, in which a line of laptops was crushed as a metaphor for the PC-crushing power found in Apple's PowerBook laptops.

PC supporters, of course, were outraged. How dare Apple make these claims? "Everyone knows Macs aren't as fast as PCs." "They must be fudging the numbers." Intel did respond, but only by posting benchmark testing on its own site to refute Apple's claims. There was no lawsuit. And by debating the issue, it simply helped Apple achieve its goal. Even if people didn't believe the numbers, they were suddenly allowing Macs into the conversation. Macs weren't quite so easy to laugh off anymore.

This was "mission accomplished" as far as Steve was concerned. He was demonstrating Apple's technical prowess and showing the world that the company was as feisty as ever. The big revolutions, starting with iMac, lay ahead.

But going to war with Intel was just a warm-up act now that Steve was back at the helm. There would be many more good fights to come.

It's Good to Have Enemies

Simplicity allows people to focus on one thing. Conversely, focusing on one thing helps achieve Simplicity. Creating a war with Intel, as Apple did, was a very effective way of getting people to focus on one thing—taking Macs seriously as a PC alternative.

Apple has a rich history of zeroing in on specific enemies, though some of those drives have worked more effectively than others. One of those moments was the campaign I mentioned in an earlier chapter, when Apple went after Microsoft, comparing the "easy way" of Macintosh to the "hard way" of Windows. But traction is difficult to establish, and this effort didn't exactly get Windows users streaming into the Apple camp.

When Steve Jobs returned to Apple in 1997, he told Apple's employees that they had to change their thinking. In another great moment for Simplicity, Steve summed it up by saying, "We have to get it out of our heads that for us to win, Microsoft has to lose." He went on to say, "The battle for the desktop is over. And we lost." Apple's enemy at that time was itself. It needed to focus all of its energy on making great products and not worry about the other guys. There would be time for that later—but only if Apple survived.

With Microsoft taken off Apple's enemies list, Steve went out of his way to embrace it as a friend. At the first Macworld following Steve's return, he announced a new partnership with Microsoft. In return for Apple dropping its ongoing lawsuit against Microsoft, Bill Gates pledged to support Microsoft Office for Mac for the next five years and invested $150 million in Apple. Some people choked at the imagery during this announcement (and groaned audibly) as Steve Jobs spoke in front of a giant screen with a video connection to Gates in Seattle. Gates appeared to be Big Brother from Apple's famous *1984* commercial, and here was Steve, cheerfully striking a deal with him. To many, it looked like surrender. Indeed, in Walter Isaacson's biography of Steve Jobs, Steve himself describes this moment as the worst presentation mistake he'd ever made. Gates's giant image looming over Steve made Microsoft seem more important than Apple.

During Steve's earliest days back at the company, many expressed doubts that even he could make things better. One such person was Michael Dell. Asked what he would do if he were CEO of Apple, he responded, "I'd shut it down and give the money back to the shareholders." Apple didn't have to go looking for that enemy—Dell carved out his own place with that gem. At an Apple event just one month later, Steve projected a large image of Michael Dell on his presentation screen, superimposing a bull's-eye target on top of it. "We're coming after you, buddy," he said. It fired up the Apple troops very well.

Choosing Intel as an enemy was an easy decision. Intel chips were the engine for all the major PC makers, and Intel was a huge advertiser with its *Intel Inside* campaign—in effect setting itself up as the proxy for the entire PC industry. Attacking Intel allowed us to attack all PC makers at once without ever mentioning a single one by name. And it got Apple attention because on the surface the claim seemed so unbelievable.

With our present-day knowledge, there's great irony in Apple singling out Intel as its enemy. Several years in the future, one of Steve's more dramatic moves would be abandoning the PowerPC platform to move to the Intel camp. When Steve made that announcement, Intel CEO Paul Otellini joined him onstage. Paul brought with him Apple's old *Burning Bunny* ad to share at the start of his speech, just to prove Intel had a sense of humor—and to show how both companies had changed since that commercial was created.

Even though Simplicity had instigated the war against Intel, moving Macs to Intel processors became a tremendous simplifier for Steve. By making the move, he completely eliminated one of the chief arguments against Apple. Suddenly Macs and PCs were at parity, enginewise. Instead of trying to dismantle old perceptions, Apple could concentrate on advertising its advantages: innovation, design, and Simplicity.

In later years, Apple would go hunting for a new enemy, and at this point it had the pleasure of recycling an old one. Just as Intel had served as a proxy for the entire PC industry before, Microsoft could fill the same bill. After all, the deal between Steve Jobs and Bill Gates had expired long ago.

The new war against Microsoft took shape in the *Mac vs. PC* campaign, which started in 2006. Through the perfectly crafted exchanges between the Mac and PC characters, the weaknesses of Windows, followed by Vista, were laid bare one by one. Viruses, crashes, upgrading problems—Apple showed no mercy. The campaign grew to be so popular, each new episode became a topic of conversation in offices and social gatherings. In fact, the popularity of the *Mac vs. PC* campaign started to hang so heavily over Microsoft, it actually responded with its own campaign, which featured a variety of people cheerfully exclaiming, "I'm a PC." Few people even remember them now—while the *Mac vs. PC* ads still pull in the views on YouTube.

What Apple has discovered over the years is that having an enemy can be fun. And if done right—quite profitable.

Use Every Available Weapon

One Sunday afternoon, I called Steve Jobs to discuss an ad that was currently in the works. He was at home, and during our conversation he got a call on his other line. He put me on hold, then returned to say, "Let me call you back in ten minutes." Click.

Sure enough, my phone rang ten minutes later. "You know who that was?" said Steve. The tone of his voice implied that (a) I'd never guess and (b) he couldn't wait to tell me.

I gave him the ceremonial "No, who?"

"That was Bill Clinton."

This would have been kind of cool even today, but at that moment Clinton was the sitting president of the United States. Steve had a good relationship with the Clintons. While the Jobs family lived in a relatively modest home, Steve had a much larger property where the Clintons would stay when they came to town for various events. It was atop a hill, with lots of land surrounding it—just the kind of setup that made the Secret Service's job easier.

The reason Clinton was calling that day was that Steve had asked for a favor, and Bill was phoning back with the result. But to appreciate Clinton's involvement, we'll have to go back to a situation that had started to play out weeks earlier.

The *Think different* campaign was in full swing, and we were running a great many magazine ads and billboards, each of which featured a single "hero." During our regular meetings with Steve every other week, we would often talk about possible new blood for the campaign.

Ideas for new heroes would come from different places. The agency was always researching new possibilities. And as the campaign became more well known, we were sometimes approached by celebrities who wanted to be a part of it. But in one meeting Steve Jobs came to the table with his own big idea: He wanted Nelson Mandela.

He talked about what an extraordinary person Mandela was and what an honor it would be to have him appear in our campaign. This wasn't some mercenary ploy to create more buzz for Apple. Steve genuinely wanted to pay tribute to a person he admired.

Only one problem. At that time, Mandela was the president of South Africa. Strain our imaginations as we could, it didn't seem likely that the leader of any country would jump at the chance to appear in an Apple ad. But we told Steve that we'd make some inquiries and see if this idea might even be in the realm of possibility. It didn't take long to get the "no thanks" back from the Mandela camp, which we promptly relayed to Steve.

Steve couldn't be angry, but he was disappointed. In keeping with the laws of Simplicity, he refused to take no for an answer. He had an idea.

"Maybe I can ask Bill Clinton if he can help," said Steve.

Right. The president. Of course. Why didn't we think of that? Steve said he'd see if Clinton could reach out to Mandela on Apple's behalf, and that was the last we heard of it for a number of days.

This brings us back to that fateful Sunday, when I was on the phone with Steve while the leader of the free world was calling on line two to report back on his homework assignment.

I couldn't ascertain whether Clinton had actually spoken with Mandela or had only reached "his people"—but again the answer was negative. As Steve explained it, Mandela might consider it one day, but only after he'd been out of office for at least six months. His intention to step down had already been made public, but the end of his presidency was still several months away.

And so the *Think different* campaign was forced to move on without the services of Nelson Mandela. Poor Nelson would have to deal with the fact that he would ultimately be replaced by someone like Charlie Chaplin. Steve continued to be disappointed, but at least he was satisfied that he'd given it the ol' presidential try.

More important, he had followed through on one of the most critical principles of Simplicity. He hadn't held back. He had used every weapon in his arsenal to work toward his goal. That he didn't succeed was not for lack of trying.

Use Overwhelming Force

If my hunch is correct, you may not have access to the president. Sadly, you may not even be able to call in a favor from the Speaker of the House.

However, what you *can* do is normally quite enough. You can make sure that when you move your ideas forward, you leave nothing to chance. This means erring on the side of overkill. By not restraining yourself, by using only the most potent weapons in your arsenal, you'll give your ideas the greatest chance of survival. Think of it as a war (because it is) and move ahead with all the grace of a military commander—by using overwhelming force.

When you're dealing with the forces of Complexity, the last thing you want is an even fight. Decisive victories are far more compelling than narrow ones. They also put a stake in the ground to influence future struggles. Bottom line: Never use a peashooter when you have access to a howitzer.

Everyone's circumstances are different, so only you know what resources you can tap. Perhaps you can make key allies in advance of a critical meeting, so you present more of a chorus than a lone voice. Perhaps there's key research or evidence that supports your point of view, which you can use to suppress arguments. Maybe you can march right into your CEO's office in search of that nod of approval that might help break up a process-inflicted logjam before it appears. Maybe you could bring in a consultant to add firepower and credibility.

Most important, you need to do everything in your power to represent your own work all the way to the top. If there were a Bill of Rights for those who generate ideas, this would likely be Article 1. When someone else represents your work to a higher level of client, or to a higher level within your own organization, only rarely will they have your level of passion. If the person representing your work runs into opposition, they'll normally be far more willing to throw in the towel than you would be, or to make compromises that you would never agree to. It's human nature.

So it must become your nature never to relent. You never want to come out even, because in this game a tie goes to Complexity. And you never want to get into an exchange of small-arms fire. There's no nicking the arm of Complexity—you need to blow it away. What's at stake is both the idea you represent and your standing in the company.

If you fail to go with overwhelming force, you are risking two things, neither of which is pleasant. First there's the greater possibility of failure. Then there are the sleepless nights you'll spend wondering what might have happened had you called in the heavy artillery.

Every new plan and every new idea needs to break through a layer of resistance. That layer could be the naysayers who don't wish to change the status quo, those who believe it can't be done, or those who simply don't have the level of commitment required to expend the effort.

Breaking through levels of resistance is easier when you use overwhelming force. Never be embarrassed to acknowledge that you can't do it by yourself. Even Steve Jobs recognized the limits of his authority. He had no problem picking up the phone to get something done—even if it was to call a guy who was busy running a country.

Simplicity: The Ultimate Weapon of War

We know that Simplicity is a fragile thing. It needs a champion to ensure that it emerges unscathed from the processes that guide any project or endeavor.

Taking on this warlike attitude helps mightily, as it will ensure that you rise above the obstacles that Complexity throws in your path. Identifying an enemy and using overwhelming force can be effective tools in your arsenal. But the point of doing all these things is to allow Simplicity to shine—because Simplicity itself is the greatest business weapon of our time.

As proof, I direct the court's attention to the launch of the original iPhone.

Putting a range of advanced capabilities literally at our fingertips, iPhone was the physical embodiment of Simplicity. It came from a company that had just proven itself with another handheld revolution. And it landed right in the middle of a category where customers were fed up with the status quo.

In other words, iPhone was a "perfect storm" of Simplicity.

Things might have been different had Apple simply been churning out Macs one day and launching a smartphone the next. But for six years leading up to iPhone, Apple had not only been successful with iPod and iTunes, it had literally changed the world. In the process, it had won the hearts of Mac and PC users alike, displaying its skill at creating handheld devices that were truly lust-inducing. Together, iPod and iTunes were life changers—opening the eyes of tens of millions of people to what Apple was capable of.

Technologically, Apple had established itself as a master of miniaturization. Philosophically, it had established itself as a master of Simplicity.

So when rumors started to appear that Apple was working on a phone, the buzz began to feed on itself. But this was no ordinary buzz. It was multiplied several times by customers' attitudes about their current phones and phone companies. Phones generally ranged from inelegant to uninspiring, and phone makers were widely perceived as monoliths that cared little about their customers. People lived with their phones, but they didn't love them. With the buzz building, iPhone wasn't just seen as a new entry in the category, it was seen as the savior—the phone that would deliver us from oppression.

The world that Apple was to invade with iPhone was dominated by BlackBerry. That product had achieved "killer" status because it did one thing well: provide access to email anywhere, anytime. Inside Apple, as was the case elsewhere, a great many depended on their BlackBerrys to stay on top of business—including those who worked on the iPhone product team.

However, as devotees of Simplicity, the Apple team could see BlackBerry's weakness clear as a bell. It was complicated. It had some good functionality—but its capabilities were nested so deeply within multiple menus, even the most tech-savvy didn't often think to use them. Apple's idea was pure Simplicity. It would create a phone that could handle phone calls and email but would also incorporate an iPod and the full Internet experience. Most important, it would make all of these capabilities so easy to use—and so obvious—that using them would seem second nature. In typical Apple fashion, the manual would be superfluous.

Given Apple's proven expertise with iPod and iTunes, a potential global market of billions (largely disgruntled customers), and a device that delivered form and function far beyond any smartphones then available, consumer electronics had never before seen such a perfect storm.

And iPhone delivered.

It was technology that would make iPhone capable, but it was Simplicity that would make it lovable. Apple had come up with a very sweet combination—and a superpowerful weapon.

This kind of power would come in handy, because Apple wasn't just going to war with a monolith called BlackBerry. It was going to war in a category filled with deep-pocketed monoliths. It would be taking on titans that had invested heavily in the status quo. These included phone makers like Motorola, LG, and Nokia, as well as the phone networks.

Soon after iPhone's launch, we saw exactly how potent a weapon Simplicity could be. The word "revolution" seems woefully inadequate. Not only was iPhone embraced by the technorati, it seduced the computer-phobic—probably because they knew how to use it before they ever picked it up. Born of Apple's love of Simplicity, iPhone didn't act like a computer, even though that's exactly what it was.

For many, iPhone was easy to fall in love with. It offered gorgeous design and amazing functionality. It was the kind of device that made you smile whenever you touched it.

Of course, iPhone was only an extension of what Apple had done throughout its history. Two years before iPhone was announced, Steve touched on the company's ability to make complicated things simple in a 2006 *Newsweek* interview:

When you first start off trying to solve a problem, the first solutions you come up with are very complex, and most people stop there. But if you keep going, and live with the problem and peel more layers of the onion off, you can oftentimes arrive at some very elegant and simple solutions.

In just a few words, Steve beautifully summed up the difference between Apple and so many other companies. Once Apple comes up with a solution, it's more of a beginning than an end. It's by peeling back those layers of Complexity that Apple is able to create its "magic."

You don't need to be creating products to apply this principle. You can use the same approach when you're creating presentations. I've yet to meet a paragraph that couldn't lose a few more words—even if it's been trimmed multiple times before. If you work harder and look more closely, there's always something you can whittle away. It's when you get to the essence of your idea that you'll have something to be proud of.

Chapter 11
Think Ahead

This new chapter appears exclusively in this paperback edition, examining Apple's commitment to Simplicity in the time since the death of Steve Jobs.

The word most frequently used to describe Steve Jobs is *visionary*.

To most people, that simply means "a person with an ability to visualize future trends."

However, visionaries come in two flavors. There are the Nostradamus types who merely report on the future they envision. And there are the Steve Jobs types who actually create the future they envision. The latter is far more rare.

Steve employed a group of brilliant designers, engineers, and marketers who, by his vision and guidance, conceived and created products that "pushed the human race forward."

Exactly how he did that will probably be studied for many years to come. But I think it's safe to say he operated by a set of values that is not "normal" for big global companies. He was willing and eager to invest millions of dollars in the pursuit of creating a great product. His decisions were based more on instinct and belief than on any true guarantee of success.

Moreover, Steve Jobs did not make profit his first priority. He was certainly proud that Apple could rake in profits at such astronomical levels.

But he believed that profits were a by-product of creating amazing computers and devices.

Apple's design chief Jony Ive echoed Steve's philosophy in a speech to London's Royal College of Art in 2010:

> *Apple's goal isn't to make money. Our goal is to design and develop and bring to market good products. We trust that as a consequence of that, we'll make some money. But we're really clear what our goals are.*

Few companies have the strength or conviction to "trust" that they will make money the way Apple does. Most set clear profit goals and then figure out how to get there. By granting itself the ability to shoot for the stars, and therefore allowing the possibility of failure, Apple makes bolder and riskier decisions—and reaps a higher profit.

Steve understood the importance of profit. He simply believed there was a better route to creating it. He would choose the most innovative course, and often passed on short-term gains to achieve even higher long-term gains. The Apple Store is a perfect example, requiring an investment of millions before the viability of the concept could be proven.

Of course, anyone who has followed Steve's career knows that his desire to invest in great ideas was his downfall at Apple in his earlier life. His willingness to pour millions into R&D, seemingly without regard to the company's financial heath, is what led John Sculley to engineer Steve's ouster.

Whatever business sense there was in driving Steve away, Apple suffered dearly in following years, as its imagination seemed to fade. Apple was the type of company that thrived as a starry-eyed startup. It didn't do so well when it dressed in a business suit.

When Steve came back in 1997, he was clearly a wiser leader and a better visionary. Apple regained its ability to innovate and began to revolutionize on a grander scale than ever before. Apple's ability to "think ahead" would soon generate profits on a scale that the younger Steve might never have imagined.

That said, no person or organization is infallible. We all make mistakes.

Before we start looking ahead for Apple, let's first acknowledge that the road is never smooth, and some things are very hard to envision—even for a visionary like Steve Jobs.

In fact, Steve once failed to recognize one of the biggest opportunities in technology history, and it happened fairly late in his career. Fortunately, he was smart enough to perform a course correction in time to revolutionize once again.

A Seriously Restrained iPhone

Love Apple or hate it, one has to admit that iPhone turned the mobile phone industry upside down. The idea of a touch-screen phone that could run a world of apps changed everything.

By mid-2012, there were over 650,000 apps in the App Store, and over 30 billion apps had been downloaded. With Apple taking a 30 percent cut of App Store purchases, apps are a huge income driver for the company.

The iPhone has been such a spectacular success that most people don't remember that the first iPhone didn't have any apps other than those that came from Apple—Weather, Stocks, Clock, etc. Publicly, Steve Jobs said that iPhone would not run third-party apps, period. Allowing that to happen would expose the device to potential corruption via viruses or unauthorized access to data.

Steve insisted that the right solution was to allow developers to create "web apps," which would run within Apple's Safari browser. In effect, they were mini web pages coded to work like apps, and they worked only when the iPhone was connected to the Internet.

Apple went so far as to focus its 2007 Worldwide Developers Conference on the craft of developing web apps for iPhone. In its press release for the event, Apple said, "Our innovative approach, using Web 2.0-based standards, lets developers create amazing new applications while keeping the iPhone secure and reliable."

This was the official company line on third-party apps. Only Apple could be trusted to protect the purity and sanctity of iPhone.

While Apple stuck to its story, developers continued to rally for the keys to the candy store. Some inside Apple agreed. Key executives tried to convince Steve that apps would open the door to a whole new world.

Though he resisted for some time, Steve ultimately changed his mind. Within a year, apps were transformed from taboo to the engine of iPhone's extraordinary growth—and one of Apple's most important sources of revenue.

Even though apps did not appear with the launch of iPhone, Apple established its App Store well before its competitors could copy it. As the library of available apps quickly grew, the size and scope of the App Store became one of iPhone's biggest selling points.

In this case, Apple's ability to think ahead was clearly limited. One might even say that Steve was trying to keep things *too* simple.

The point is, as Apple moves forward without Steve, it will no doubt stumble from time to time—just as it did *with* Steve. Innovation is a somewhat bumpy road, and the company's first year without Steve had its shaky moments.

Moving Forward Without the Founder

The more successful Apple becomes, the more intensely it is scrutinized. The fact that Steve passed away in the very year that Apple become the world's most valuable company has led many observers to ask "What now?"

Can Apple continue on its stellar path without Steve to guide it? Have Steve's values been sufficiently instilled into the company? Can new CEO Tim Cook make high-stakes decisions as effectively as Steve did?

As always, the over-analysis of Apple can lead to erroneous conclusions. It's best if we just start with the obvious: Steve Jobs was unique. It is simply not possible for Apple to be the same company without him.

Steve provided leadership in many areas, including vision, engineering, design, and marketing. Since no one person can replace him, he needs to be replaced by a number of people. The good news is, Steve surrounded himself with brilliant people, and the executive team is largely intact. They understand what sets Apple apart, and they're not about to abandon Apple's values.

Though one year isn't a lot of time to judge Apple's ability to perform without Steve, most of the signs are positive. In 2012, Apple launched quite a few new products, including iPhone 5, two new generations of iPad, iPad mini, a new family of iPods, and a redesigned family of iMacs.

As he demonstrated during his tenure as COO, Tim Cook has a major talent for operations, and he proved that by successfully managing so many product introductions in the fall of 2012. All key products overcame initial backlogs and were shipping without issues well before the holidays.

However, the year following Steve's death has not been without controversy—and of course many Apple observers can't stop themselves from directly connecting the controversies to Steve's absence.

Most notorious was the debacle caused by the introduction of Apple Maps. With iOS 6 and iPhone 5, Apple replaced Google Maps in favor of its own mapping product. While many see this as an example of Apple shooting itself in the foot, the truth is more complicated than that.

The first iteration of Apple Maps was indeed flawed. Almost within minutes of its debut, reports flowed in about inaccurate and missing addresses—not exactly the best publicity for a feature that people rely on to go from one place to another. It got worse with each passing day, as more and more major glitches were discovered. Entire geographic areas were missing and landmarks misplaced.

Tim Cook's reaction to the rapidly escalating problem demonstrated that he is no longer in the shadow of Steve Jobs. He apologized—very publicly—with an open letter on Apple's website. He admitted that Apple had "fallen short" of its commitment to create great products. He not only promised that things would get better, he went on to suggest alternatives to Apple Maps as Apple worked to improve its product. I don't believe we've ever seen Apple recommend that people choose another company's product over one of its own.

This, of course, raises a few juicy questions.

Would Steve Jobs ever have delivered such an outright apology? Does this make Tim a better or worse leader than Steve? Would Steve ever have allowed Apple Maps to be released in the first place? Of course, it's impossible to answer such questions. Especially when Steve himself made a number of misjudgments over his career.

During the iPhone 4 "Antennagate" controversy—when users complained that holding an iPhone 4 in a certain way would cause reception problems or calls to be dropped completely—Steve took the unprecedented measure of calling a press conference. His presentation was more of a defense than an admission of guilt. He certainly never apologized to the degree that Cook did. He shared a stack of evidence proving that all phones suffer from similar issues. He showed off Apple's advanced research facilities. His "apology" was simply an offer to give every iPhone 4 owner a free bumper case that would eliminate the problem. He never admitted that Apple had "fallen short" as Cook did. In fact, he did the opposite. He tried to prove that Apple was leading the way in telephone design.

The truth is, Apple had solid business reasons to part ways with Google, who has turned into the company's chief competitor with its Android technology. For years, Steve had made the point that Apple couldn't allow itself to depend on other companies to define the Apple user experience. When Adobe fell on its face trying to create a version of Flash that worked well enough on iPhone, Steve dumped Flash and moved to the emerging open standard of HTML5. He would never again allow Apple to depend on another company to provide a critical function or service.

Now here was Google controlling a critical part of Apple's iOS. There was one year remaining on Apple's agreement with Google to use Google Maps on iPhone and iPad. Google was not giving iPhone users turn-by-turn directions, even though Android phones had been enjoying that feature for two years. iPhone customers weren't getting the best experience and Android was getting a competitive advantage.

Thus, Apple found itself in a "damned if you do, damned if you don't" situation. It could suffer through another year with a lesser-featured Google Maps app, or it could create its own app that would include turn-by-turn directions and offer features that Google Maps didn't, such as 3-D flyovers.

However, the debate over what Apple should do would certainly include the assumption that Apple Maps would be a comparable product from the start—which it was not. So, it's hard to excuse Apple for choosing the course it did. Clearly Apple tests products in the field, and it had to be obvious that its Maps function was seriously flawed. This raises nagging questions about who knew what, and when.

Comparing Tim Cook's handling of the Apple Maps controversy to Steve Jobs's handling of Antennagate, it's revealing that Cook never bothered to put the Maps decision in a business context. He simply apologized, and did so with gusto. One can assume that he wanted the apology to be genuine without appearing to offer excuses. There was nothing for the critics to refute.

This is actually an interesting exercise in Simplicity.

Rather than make a big deal of it, Tim decided to just acknowledge the issue, restate Apple's high quality standards, and tell the world that fixing Maps was a high priority.

It appears that Tim's strategy worked. Most of the responses to his apology were positive, citing the human quality of Tim's words. Public discussion of Maps' deficiencies faded rather quickly, and now Apple must deliver the solution in a timely fashion—or face renewed criticism at a future date.

Unfortunately, Maps was not Apple's only lapse in 2012.

A Less-Than-Genius Ad Campaign

Certain televised events are considered terrific stages for advertisers—prime time for new campaigns to be unveiled. The Super Bowl, the Oscars, and the World Series are the more obvious examples.

The Olympic Games, broadcast every two years, are also a premium buy. Because they go on for a longer period of time, there's plenty of room for advertisers to play—and to spend huge sums of money unveiling their big advertising moments.

During the Summer Olympics of 2012, Apple bought a large presence. It produced a new campaign for its Mac products (the first since killing the supersuccessful *Mac vs. PC* campaign). This is not the type of thing a company does lightly. The cost is huge, so the plans must be made far in advance. More often than not, ads that debut on the Olympics continue to have a shelf life afterward. That way, their cost can be better justified.

Apple's new effort was the *Genius* campaign. It consisted of three commercials, each featuring a young, supposedly engaging Genius from the Apple Store. The idea of the campaign was that even when the Genius wasn't at work, he would find himself in situations where he would save the day for an Apple customer who needed help—on a plane, in his apartment building, on the street.

The campaign bombed. It was quickly attacked in the blogosphere, for a number of good reasons.

First, it wasn't very funny. The exaggerated characters came off like sitcom actors. Or, more accurately, they came off as sitcom actors reading unfunny scripts. The quality of the commercials seemed shockingly beneath Apple's usually high standards.

But there was another, possibly more disturbing, problem. Since the beginning of time, Apple's advantage has been that its products are easy to use. They make it easy for us ordinary folk to do some very cool things. In this new campaign, every ad showed us another person who couldn't figure out things on their own. We met them in varying degrees of panic and in serious need of help.

The result was something unprecedented in Apple's history. Following the public outcry, after just a few weeks, the ads were taken off the air. The company issued a statement indicating that the ads were designed to run only for a limited time and that they had run their course.

However, the facts demonstrated how Apple really felt about this campaign. Not only did the ads cease to run, they were pulled from Apple's website—where ads would normally remain for some time. They were also pulled from Apple's YouTube channel, where ads would normally remain far longer. Anyone who had posted the ads on their own YouTube channel found them removed due to copyright violations.

Clearly Apple wasn't happy with the ads. And just in case anyone ever wanted to talk about them again—the evidence was destroyed.

This was a situation where the ads did not live up to Apple's standards, and the company's reaction to public criticism was more suspicious than honest. Fortunately, life does go on. Flawed advertising isn't nearly as bad as flawed products. These ads faded from public consciousness rather quickly once they stopped running, just as Apple appeared to hope.

However, this failed campaign provided strong new evidence to those making the case that Apple was on the downslope following Steve's death. Since Steve had been actively involved in all advertising, the *Genius* campaign was immediately greeted by the "Steve would never have approved that" argument.

From personal experience, I know that Steve often vetoed the opinions of his most senior marketing people. Obviously, without Steve in the room some things that deserve to be vetoed will not be. But no one can say for sure how he might have ruled in any one case.

I was surprised that Apple had created a campaign that was deficient in so many ways. You can criticize it on many levels, but the bottom line is that a lot of people just didn't like it. If your company is going to spend millions of dollars to leave an impression with customers, it's always a good thing if those impressions are positive.

Defenders of the campaign point out that these ads were designed to comfort new users and that more advanced users were not the target. If you know advertising, you know that's an awful argument. The previous Mac campaign, *Mac vs. PC*, was phenomenally successful. It was also aimed at new users, but it delighted the more experienced customers as well. In fact, it turned them into evangelists, as they would use those ads to bolster their arguments to friends and colleagues. A great campaign does not alienate one group as it targets another.

While I was personally disappointed in the *Genius* campaign, I didn't see it as a sign of Apple's impending doom. Despite the best of intentions, a new campaign can come off the rails anywhere along the production process. The nature of creativity is that when you shoot for the stars, sometimes you miss. To me, the real test was going to be the campaign that followed. If Apple produced two clunkers in a row, then I'd be concerned.

But Apple never looked back. The iPhone 5 campaign that followed was arguably Apple's best advertising in years. These new ads featured actor Jeff Daniels in the voiceover role—quirky, intelligent, and likable. In my opinion, this campaign was actually better than most of the iPhone ads created under Steve Jobs. They beautifully reflected Apple's love of Simplicity, with each ad explaining a single iPhone 5 feature with simple, often charming images.

Following the debut of this campaign came a campaign for another new product, iPad mini. These ads were even simpler, featuring a point/counterpoint between two side-by-side iPads—one regular and one mini. They made you smile, and they unmistakably delivered their message: now there's a smaller iPad.

So the marketing alarm bells remain silent. Apple's stellar record of advertising did experience a blip with the *Genius* campaign, but order was restored with the iPhone 5 campaign and iPad mini campaign that soon followed. Whoever was responsible for the *Genius* campaign no doubt had their wrists slapped or experienced something a bit more severe.

Apple's advertising, like its product design, will continue on its path of quality as long as its stewards remain true to the company's core values.

Tim Rights a Wrong

In late 2012, Tim Cook made his boldest move yet. He shook up the Apple executive team.

The first move was a no-brainer. John Browett, who had been brought in to replace Ron Johnson as head of the Apple Stores, was fired. He had been blasted in the press for what appeared to be a terribly bone-headed move.

His goal seemed to be increasing profits in the Apple Stores, and he planned to do that by curtailing employees' hours.

I say "bone-headed" because even the most casual observer can see that customer service is the number one draw in the Apple Stores, and the stores are immensely profitable already (most recently, over $5 billion in annual profits). Prioritizing profit over customer service seems wrong in every possible way. Even worse, it seems very un-Apple.

Of course, in this case Cook was simply fixing a mistake he had made himself. Browett was his choice to head the retail effort, even though many looked at that decision with doubt when it was announced. Browett came from the Dixons retail chain in Europe, which seemed to be a world away from Apple's values.

A far more shocking move was the dismissal of Scott Forstall. Scott was a personal favorite of Steve Jobs going all the way back to NeXT and was in charge of the iOS software platform. iOS, powering iPhone and iPad, is the most visible and most critical software group within modern-day Apple.

Scott was seen by many to share certain qualities with Steve. He could be abrasive and aggressive, though he was obviously good at getting things done. One might pause to make an observation about the way human beings react to one another. People accepted Steve Jobs behavior in Steve Jobs. They had a tough time accepting it in anyone else.

Scott's role within Apple became more critical as iOS became a core driver of Apple's business. With Steve's backing, certain features from iOS were being incorporated into OS X, giving users more consistency between computers and devices.

And therein lay the problem.

The Great Skeuomorphism Debate

For some time, rumors were circulating that Apple's designer-in-chief, Jony Ive, was not a fan of Scott Forstall. It had gotten so bad that Jony reportedly refused to attend meetings when Scott was present.

Clearly there was a personality issue there. Scott's aggressive style did not jibe well with Jony's more gentlemanly British style. But there was also a design issue causing a rift between them. It's called *skeuomorphism*.

In the world of computer interfaces, a skeuomorph is the ornamental design on an interface element that harks back to a familiar real-world object, thus making its purpose obvious. Simple examples would be the folder and trash can on the computer desktop, or a thermometer icon that represents a weather app.

In Scott Forstall's world, skeuomorphism was starting to go places that made many designers cringe. On the iPhone and iPad, for example, iBooks appeared on a wooden bookshelf that looked very dated. And now OS X was being infected with this type of interface design, as Apple consciously brought iOS features into the Mac world.

Suddenly the Calendar app in OS X Lion looked like grandpa's old desktop blotter. The Contacts app also sported a leather design. The Notes app presented itself as a yellow note pad, complete with bits of torn paper at the top. OS X had always been known for its simple and elegant interface, and now it was being cluttered with these skeuomorphic exercises, and there was no way for a user to make them go away. Worse yet, there was little consistency to it. Calendar and Contacts went the leather route, but other everyday apps like Reminders and Dictionary remained clean.

Some debated whether skeuomorphs have any place in a modern interface, since most of today's users have grown up with technology and don't need the comforts of real-world references. Others had no problem with skeuomorphs in general, but questioned why Apple's skeuomorphs were referencing things that none of us ever even used (like the leather desk blotter).

No doubt Jony was frustrated that his beautifully designed hardware was being taken down a notch by screens that contained outdated or cheesy skeuomorphs.

More important, the rift between Forstall and Ive highlighted a serious problem growing within Apple. Since the first Macintosh was born, one of Apple's most highly touted advantages had been its perfect integration of hardware and software. It was all made to work together beautifully. Yet the heads of two key divisions—hardware and iOS—were now at odds with each other. They didn't agree on major design issues, and there was no camaraderie between them. Integration between hardware and software, at least on the design level, was not being served.

Tim Cook's bold shakeup solved this problem once and for all. With Forstall sent packing, Cook gave Jony Ive the additional responsibility of Human Interface across all Apple products.

This is a huge and happy development for Apple's commitment to Simplicity. Now one sense of design will carry over from hardware to software in every computer and device that Apple builds. There will be more consistency between different devices.

And I strongly suspect that your calendar will soon emerge from its leather wrapping.

A Forward-Thinking Apple

Despite a few scares here and there, Apple has largely conducted business as usual without Steve. And business as usual for Apple remains unusual in the general marketplace.

This is good. It's when Apple starts acting like everyone else that AAPL shareholders should seriously consider cashing out.

Tim Cook's recent executive shakeup alone is proof that Apple continues to think ahead, envisioning what their products will look like for many years to come. Simplicity, elegance, and consistency will clearly be the guiding lights.

There will always be rumors of new Apple products, such as the Apple television rumor that has floated around for more than a year. It's telling that however people imagine these products to work, they always imagine that Apple will revolutionize the category by bringing a refreshing Simplicity.

That's how they perceive Apple's talent. That's the expectation that Apple seeks to fulfill.

Apple's existing products continue to represent the company's brand image well, as evidenced by iPhone 5, a crop of new iPads, and more. The marketing continues to excel, despite one flawed moment. And, happily, a growing rift between hardware and software design has been repaired, indicating a positive trend forward.

The power of Simplicity endures.

Conclusion
Think Different

When you believe in the power of Simplicity, you are by definition "thinking different." You're in the minority. Simplicity may be one of the most powerful forces on earth, but it is the weapon of the few.

From a business point of view, this is actually very good news. Being a rare commodity, Simplicity has greater value. Companies that leverage its power can stand out from their competitors. Individuals who master it become greater assets to their organizations.

Simplicity Is Always Original

Before you begin practicing your Simplicity skills out in the real world, you need to be mindful of one important fact: A simple idea is not necessarily a better idea. Quality counts.

If you start with something truly fresh and compelling, then applying the principles of Simplicity can take you to fantastic heights. However, a bad idea remains bad no matter how you try to simplify it. And unfortunately, being a believer in Simplicity does not exempt you from having bad ideas.

Apple, despite having proven itself a bastion of Brains and Common Sense, has made some historic blunders. Some were bad ideas to start with; others were good ideas gone bad. Fortunately for Apple, the company has a rather nice insurance policy: over $120 billion in cash reserves (as of October 2012). As I once heard Steve Jobs explain it, this is what gives Apple the freedom to make such imaginative leaps. It has the comforting knowledge that if things don't go right, it'll always land on solid ground.

Since most of us don't even have a single billion in the bank, it's nice to know that Simplicity offers its own backup plan. By adhering to its principles, you'll find that it's easier to recover from mistakes, and sometimes emerge even stronger.

The Mouse That Didn't Roar

One of Apple's best-known failures is the "hockey puck mouse" that shipped with the original iMac and the Power Mac G3 that soon followed. Even die-hard Apple fans hated it. It was round—and the problem with round is that you can't tell which way it's pointed. So people sitting down to do some work often found their on-screen cursors moving around in unexpected directions. Why Apple never figured this out before shipping it is a mystery. The hockey puck mouse gave critics more fodder to argue that Apple was obsessed with form over function.

A few months into the hockey puck mouse's life, before a Macworld event in New York, Steve Jobs invited me up to his Manhattan hotel room to go over some ads in progress. After we had finished the review, we got to talking about other things, and I couldn't resist bringing up the mouse. It was on my mind because the press was getting nastier, and as an iMac user myself, I had given up on it and bought a more usable mouse.

I gave Steve some of the brutal honesty he appreciated. I told him that the brand was really taking a hit because of this adventure. But what really bothered me was how we were treating the pro users. It was bad enough to give this mouse to the iMac buyers (who were mostly home users), but those who bought the Power Mac G3 were pros. To them, this simply was a nonstarter. A mouse this clumsy just wouldn't be an acceptable tool for people who spend entire days finessing their work.

"I think this mouse is actually an insult to the pro users," I said.

There was a short period of silence as Steve sat there, unsmiling. For a second I thought I'd overstepped my bounds. Then, expressionless, he looked me in the eye and said: "Fuck 'em."

He let me stew on that for a second or two—then he started laughing. He loved his customers, pro and otherwise, and he was just having a little fun with my moment of discomfort. He knew darn well that Apple had made a mistake, and the company had started working on a replacement mouse immediately. Then the boyish, excited Steve kicked in and started telling me about the new mouse. It was going to be awesome, a transparent laser mouse that was superaccurate. The pros—and everyone else—would be delighted with it. Apple had already moved way beyond its mistake, even if the solution hadn't been made public yet.

In an interview, Steve Jobs once said:

Sometimes when you innovate, you make mistakes. It is best to admit them quickly, and get on with improving your other innovations.

Simplicity doesn't like to get tangled up in old problems. It vastly prefers to look ahead. Though it may be painful to admit mistakes, customers appreciate this kind of honesty. When the new mouse was unveiled, the hockey puck mouse became a distant memory.

The Power Mac G4 Cube was another of Apple's classic blunders—even though it was such a marvelously designed system that it became part of the Museum of Modern Art's permanent collection. The problem with the Cube was that it was just too expensive. Try as they might, Apple's engineers couldn't get the price low enough. Steve received this news immediately before one of our regular agency meetings, and he was visibly shaken by it. He had poured his heart into the G4 Cube in the hope that it would be affordable for consumers, but instead it would have to be priced more like a pro machine. In his depression, he acknowledged that this could easily lead to failure for this product. And indeed, he ended up killing the G4 Cube just a year after he unveiled it.

This was another example of Apple acting with great speed to fix a problem and move on. The G4 Cube became a blip in Apple's history, and the vacuum it left was quickly filled by other innovations.

Like Money in the Brand Bank

It's because a company is likely to experience both success and failure along its trajectory that Steve Jobs was a firm believer in the concept of the "brand bank."

He believed that a company's brand works like a bank account. When the company does good things, such as launch a hit product or a great campaign, it makes deposits in the brand bank. When a company experiences setbacks, like an embarrassing mouse or an overpriced computer, it's making a withdrawal. When there's a healthy balance in the brand bank, customers are more willing to ride out the tough times. With a low balance, they might be more tempted to cut and run.

Steve went on record many times about the importance of building a strong Apple brand. And he benefited from having a high balance in the brand bank many times. One of the most negative stories in recent years was the now-famous "Antennagate" controversy. When iPhone 4 was launched, Apple was battered by journalists and influential bloggers over what was perceived to be a flawed antenna design. Despite the heavily negative press and ridiculing by late-night TV hosts, Apple's customers remained true. Now that episode is remembered only as an example of overreaction, with virtually no long-term impact.

An even more serious controversy erupted with the introduction of iPhone 5 and iOS 6, when Apple replaced Google Maps with its own mapping system. Apple Maps was quickly found to be inaccurate and incomplete. But with an apology from CEO Tim Cook and a promise to improve the product quickly, again Apple seems to have suffered no long-term harm.

Having a high balance in the brand bank makes all the difference.

Harnessing the Power of Simplicity

What Apple has accomplished in just the last ten years is almost hard to fathom.

They're a band of brilliant engineers, designers, manufacturers, and marketers performing miracles through a rare combination of technology skills, artistic sensibility, and sheer bravado. They hold themselves up to absurdly high standards, demanding perfection in every last detail.

So, can Simplicity help you build the next Apple? Not unless you have a few thousand of the industry's best people on call. Can Simplicity help you achieve spectacular results for your business? Absolutely. That's because Simplicity is not the goal—it's the guiding light that can help a business achieve its goals. It's when you apply the principles of Simplicity to your job, and to your company's business processes, that you'll appreciate its power.

This is what Apple has done. It's embraced a concept that has such elemental power, it can successfully be applied to every discipline within the company. What Apple does is beyond difficult—but it succeeds because it is unrelenting in its devotion to Simplicity.

As a proponent of Simplicity, your goals should definitely be lofty. There's no reason why Simplicity can't help power your company to great heights and help you build a skill that puts you in greater demand.

Since human beings are predisposed toward Simplicity, every one of us has the ability to tap into this power. Now that you've seen how Apple adheres to the elements of Simplicity, it's time to start thinking about some practical means for you to do the same:

Think Brutal. No need to be mean, just brutally honest—and avoid the partial truths while you're at it. Ask those you interact with to do the same. People will be more focused, more positive, and more productive when they don't have to guess what you're thinking. Positive or negative, make honesty the basis of all interactions. You'll avoid wasting valuable time and energy later.

Think Small. Swear allegiance to the concept of small groups of smart people. Remember it well when new project groups are formed. This is a key component of Simplicity, and you must become its champion. Small groups of smart people deliver better results, higher efficiency, and improved morale. Also, look suspiciously at any project plan that doesn't include the regular participation of the final decision maker. It's critical. Having the decision maker appear at the very end of the process to say yea or nay is a recipe for frustration and mediocrity.

Think Minimal. Be mindful of the fact that every time you attempt to communicate more than one thing, you're splintering the attention of those you're talking to—whether they're customers or colleagues. If it's necessary to deliver multiple messages, find a common theme that unites them all and push hard on that idea. You want people to remember what you say—and the more you cram into your communication, the more difficult you make it for them.

Remember that a sea of choices is no choice at all. The more you can minimize your proposition, the more attractive it will be.

Think Motion. The perfect project timeline is only slightly less elusive than the Holy Grail. It takes some effort to figure it out, but once you do, you'll have created a template that promotes success. You may not be the person tasked with creating timelines, but you can try to influence those who are. This is the kind of thing that most people just accept, but they shouldn't. The right timing is as important as the right people. Always be wary of the "comfortable" timeline—it's just a fact of life that a degree of pressure keeps things moving ahead with purpose. With too much time in the schedule, you're just inviting more opinions, and more opportunities to have your ideas nibbled to death. Keep things in motion at all times.

Think Iconic. Even if you're not in the marketing biz, it will serve you well to crystallize your thinking by leveraging an image that can symbolize your idea, or the spirit of it. And if you are in the marketing business, you're simply required by law to think this way. Whatever presentations you make, whatever products you sell, whomever you're trying to convince—never forget the power of an image to galvanize your audience. Note that there's a big difference between finding a great image and decorating a PowerPoint presentation. There's too much decorating in the world already, and for the most part it's meaningless. Find a conceptual image that actually captures the essence of your idea. Be simple and be strong.

The same principle applies whether you're talking to colleagues or to the public. Over time, a conceptual image gives people an easy way to identify your company, your idea or your product. Memorable images often communicate more effectively than words—which is why those who value Simplicity tend to rely on them.

Think Phrasal. This is an area where just about every business needs more work. Words are powerful, but more words are not more powerful—they're often just confusing. Understand that in your company's internal business and in communications with your customers, dissertations don't necessarily prove smarts. In fact, they tend to drive people away.

Though many writers never seem to grasp the point, using intelligent words does not necessarily make you appear smarter. The best way to make yourself or your company look smart is to express an idea simply and with perfect clarity. No matter who your audience is, it's more effective to communicate as people do naturally. In simple sentences. Using simple words. Simplicity is its own form of cleverness—saying a great deal by saying little.

Apple's website is a primer for intelligence in communications. There is a cleverness in writing that runs throughout, but much of the feeling of Apple's "smarts" comes from its brevity and straightforwardness. In a world where too many people are trying too hard, Simplicity can be extremely refreshing.

The same can be said for product naming. Simple and natural names stick with people, while jargon and model numbers do not. If you wish people to form a relationship with your product, it needs a name people can naturally associate with. Product naming is one area in which Simplicity pays immediate returns.

Think Casual. Do what Steve Jobs did: Shun the trappings of big business. Operating like a smaller, less hierarchical company makes everyone more productive—and makes it more likely that you'll become a bigger business. Choreographed meetings and formalized presentations may transfer information from person to person, but they neither inspire nor bring a team closer together. Embrace the fact that you'll get more accomplished when you converse with people rather than present to them. You'll still have plenty of opportunities to dress up and do things the old-fashioned way. But internally, and on a day-to-day basis with your clients—deformalize.

Many great creative ideas are actually born in these types of briefings, when key words or phrases emerge in conversation. Some of the agency's most compelling words for Apple were generated this way. If you want to reap the benefits of Simplicity, think big—but don't act that way. As Steve Jobs proved, one of the most effective ways to become a big business is to maintain the culture of a small business.

Think Human. Unless you're in the business of sterilizing things, business is no place to be sterile. Have the boldness to look beyond numbers and spreadsheets and allow your heart to have a say in the matter. Bear in mind that the intangibles are every bit as real as the metrics— oftentimes even more important. The simplest way—and most effective way—to connect with human beings is to speak with a human voice. It may be necessary in your business to market to specific target groups, but bear in mind that every target is a human being, and human beings respond to Simplicity.

Think Skeptic. Expect the first reaction of others to be negative. The forces of Complexity will inevitably tell you that something can't be done, even if the truth is that your request simply requires extra effort. You'll probably achieve better results if you believe more in the talent of people to work miracles than in those who are quick to provide negative answers.

Don't allow the discouragement of others to force compromise upon your ideas. Push. If you can't get satisfaction with one person or vendor, move to another. If there was one area in which Steve Jobs had a well-deserved reputation for being impossible, this was it. He was relentless about executing ideas and demanding that people perform.

Take pride in your independence and objectivity too. See facts and opinions in context. Definitely consider the expertise of those who provide counsel, but evaluate those opinions against things that may be beyond the expert's vision—like your long-term goals. Steve Jobs knew that the short-term cost, even if it's large, is often outweighed by the future benefit. Real leaders have the ability to grasp the context and decide accordingly. Simplicity isn't afraid to act on Common Sense, even when it runs counter to an expert's opinion.

Think War. Extreme times call for extreme measures. When your ideas are facing life or death, that's an extreme time. Like a soldier in battle, you can't afford to suffer even a single hit—so make sure you hit first. Pull out all the stops. Remember, when your idea's life is on the line, the last thing you want is a fair fight. Use every available weapon. If possible, grab the unfair advantage. And never forget what might well be your most effective weapon: the passion you feel for your idea.

Spreading the Religion of Simplicity

It's natural for people to be resistant to change, large or small, so trying to change attitudes within an organization can be difficult. However, Steve Jobs's legacy will make your effort easier.

Steve created such a remarkable organization, and achieved such spectacular success, that he gained the respect of even his fiercest competitors. His accomplishments are not only fascinating to those in technology and marketing—they're fascinating to those in just about every industry. That's because pretty much the whole world has been impacted by Apple innovations, and Steve's life was a remarkable news story in itself.

So when you spread the word about the value of Simplicity, you're not spreading some oddball theory espoused by an obscure management guru—you're talking about a powerful tool wielded by one of the most successful and important people in business history. If you refer to the benefits Apple has enjoyed by embracing Simplicity and make the appropriate parallels to your own business, you'll build a compelling case.

You can spread the religion of Simplicity project by project, by interacting with people and groups one at a time. Even better is to organize a group or companywide meeting to talk about how your organization can leverage the power of Simplicity. In this type of meeting, you can rally the troops and ask them to contribute ideas for simplifying the organization in any way possible, from standard office policies to the way project teams are created and empowered, from the way products and services are created and evolved to the way your company interacts with clients. Forcing people to follow new rules is always an uphill battle, but getting them to buy into a concept to the point where they start contributing their own ideas can literally create a movement within an organization.

Simplicity can be contagious. Once you get people turned on to its advantages, it really can become an obsession—just as it did with history-making results for Apple.

Steve Jobs's Monument to Simplicity

As Apple demonstrates, Simplicity can take many forms. It can be an idea or a finished product. It can be the inspiration or the end result, or the process that leads from one to the other.

That's because Simplicity is a concept more than any one thing. It's a way of looking at every part of your job, the jobs of those around you, and the way your entire company operates. Once you start seeing the world through the lens of Simplicity, you'll be astounded at how many opportunities exist to improve the way your business works.

You can hit selected parts of your business with the Simple Stick. But the real power of Simplicity is felt when, as happened with Apple, it becomes a companywide obsession. It's the combined effect of multiple parts of the company being guided by Simplicity that has powered Apple in its miraculous rise from the ashes. Steve instilled the religion of Simplicity deep into the soul of the company, so that Apple could continue to thrive for many years to come.

In this sense, Steve's greatest achievement wasn't a Mac, iPod, iPhone, or iPad. He accomplished something that no one had even contemplated before. Steve Jobs built a monument to Simplicity.

That monument is Apple itself.

Apple is both a testament to the power of Simplicity and a blueprint for those who wish to follow it. Simplicity requires only your understanding, commitment, and passion—though a certain degree of Jobs-style relentlessness will greatly assist.

It will be a challenge, because you live and work in a complicated world. But it will be fruitful for the very same reason. In a world where Complexity abounds, those who stand up for Simplicity will always stand apart.

Happy simplification.

"Simple can be harder than complex. You have to work hard to get your thinking clean to make it simple. But it's worth it in the end, because once you get there, you can move mountains."

—Steve Jobs

Acknowledgments

This book has been percolating for a decade or two, even if I didn't know it. I owe a debt of gratitude to all those who opened the doors and opened my eyes.

First on my list is Steve Jobs. I thank him for not throwing me out of the room when we met, even though he didn't have the opportunity to interview me first. Had that gone differently, this book would be about my adventures writing insurance ads.

Another big thanks to Lee Clow, chief of TBWA\Chiat\Day, who gave me the opportunity to serve as Steve's creative director. That was my fourth tour of duty at the agency, and if Lee had seen enough of me after number three, this book would also not exist.

But I wouldn't be thanking Steve Jobs or Lee Clow if it weren't for Steve Hayden. He's the one who first gave me a chance to work on Apple when he moved from Chiat to BBDO in the John Sculley era. Years later, he brought me into the IBM world at Ogilvy. Steve is the original voice of Apple and my god of copywriting.

The circumstances that led directly to this book came together in more recent times.

We can blame Valerie Hausladen, my former colleague in Austin, for asking me to help her create a blog—which inspired me to start my own blog. She then asked if I would edit her book, *Professional Destiny*—which inspired me to write my own book. If that weren't enough, it was Valerie who suggested that I attend Book Expo in New York, where the plot thickened.

My wonderful and insightful neighbor, Sara Schneider, who was then in the publishing business (but came to her senses and transitioned into the cupcake business), told me to stop by at her company's booth at the Book Expo. By sheer coincidence, she ended up introducing me to business book expert Todd Sattersten, who was intrigued by my idea and offered his guidance. Todd knows so much about this business, it's frightening.

One thing Todd knows is terrific agents—and he led me directly to literary agent Christy Fletcher, who has been enthusiastic and supportive since the first day we met. Though I remember little of that meeting due to the jackhammers outside her office window.

It was Christy who then connected me with the team at Portfolio, starting with publisher Adrian Zackheim. Adrian sparked to my idea, and made me instantly feel like Portfolio was my kind of place—which it turned out to be in every possible way.

I owe a huge, huge thanks to editor Courtney Young. Her ability to shape and refine thoughts across tens of thousands of words is pretty remarkable. Brilliance aside, she also had the ability to save me from myself.

There are many more to thank at Portfolio, including Amanda Pritzker in publicity, Eric Meyers, and the whole design team, all of whom have been amazingly supportive.

A big thank-you is also due to my insanely enthusiastic publicist Angela Hayes and her associates at Goldberg McDuffie.

And there are others without whose help, patience, and guidance this book would have sputtered long ago.

Michael Rylander and Tom Witt have acted as my creative partners, close friends, and conscience for over twenty years, going all the way back to our days on NeXT. Michael was instrumental in designing various parts of this book, while Tom spent way too many days of his life reading and offering his sage advice. Both helped reconstruct some of the more obscure memories in these pages.

Stephen Sonnenfeld has been a colleague for years, and we've fought in the trenches together on IBM, Intel, and Dell. I thank him for contributing his memories and analysis to this book.

My sister, Zita Segall Neto, a language expert in Portugal, acted as my personal 24/7 English Crisis Line. She was a truly invaluable resource. My brother, Norm, heads up the *Insanely Simple* legal team and is on call to get me out of jail.

Allen Olivo, Apple's chief marketer during the *Think different* days, was a fellow soldier during a challenging and wonderful time, and proved to be an excellent jogger of memories.

Rob Kell, an Austin designer with a Los Angeles soul, served as my creative sounding board, a pair of fresh eyes, and a shoulder to cry on.

Stan Slap, author of *Bury My Heart at Conference Room B*, graciously gave of his time to help me understand the dark art of book writing and promoting.

Last, a super thank-you to my wife, Susan, and son, Jeremy, who had reason to believe I was on the other side of that closed door but saw little proof of it over the last year or so. But they did get to go on vacation without me, so maybe we're even. Note to both: You have amazing patience and I look forward to getting to know you again sometime.

There are many more whose support and feedback helped make this book possible, and I am truly grateful to all.

Ken

Index